COMPACT AKTIV-TEST

# 2.000 x
# Minuten-Training
# ENGLISH
# Conversation

Isabel Barlage
Mark Jordan

---

Compact Verlag

Redaktion: Bea Herrmann, Karina Partsch
Redaktionsassistenz: Johanna Kappelmann
Produktionsleitung: Uwe Eckhard
Umschlaggestaltung: Inga Koch
Printed in Germany
ISBN 3-8174-7133-5
7271332

Besuchen Sie uns im Internet: www.compactverlag.de

# Vorwort

Der praktische Compact Aktiv-Test ermöglicht es Ihnen, Ihre Konversationsfähigkeiten im Englischen schnell und auf einfache Weise zu vertiefen, aufzufrischen und zu überprüfen.

Die kurzweiligen Übungen in einem handlichen Format machen den Aktiv-Test zur idealen Trainingsmöglichkeit für zwischendurch – ob in Bus oder Bahn, an der Haltestelle, im Wartezimmer, in der Mittagspause oder zu Hause.

Mit 2.000 Einzelübungen umfasst das Buch die wichtigsten und gebräuchlichsten Vokabeln und Redewendungen der englischen Konversation.

Schreiben Sie Ihre Lösungen einfach ins Buch! Die richtigen Lösungen sind stets auf der gegenüberliegenden Seite angegeben.

Mit dem Compact Aktiv-Test und einem Bleistift haben Sie die Grundausrüstung, um Ihre Englischkenntnisse in Minutenschnelle zu trainieren. Viel Spaß!

# Inhalt

Lösung 1: a. introduce b. What c. Can d. like e. meet f. Where g. Could h. living i. occupation j. Good k. evening/afternoon l. How m. well n. glad o. things

## 1. Meet & Greet Was passt in die Lücken?

a. Can I _ _ _ _ _ _ _ you to my friend Michael?
b. Hello. My name's Mark. _ _ _ _ _ _ _ is yours?
c. _ _ _ _ _ _ _ I introduce you to my friend Margaret?
d. I'd _ _ _ _ _ _ _ you to meet my neighbour Tom.
e. Pleased to _ _ _ _ _ _ _ you.
f. I'm from Celbridge. _ _ _ _ _ _ _ are you from?
g. _ _ _ _ _ _ _ you tell me your name please?
h. What do you do for a _ _ _ _ _ _ _ ?
i. Do you have an _ _ _ _ _ _ _ ?
j. _ _ _ _ _ _ _ morning.
k. Good _ _ _ _ _ _ _ .
l. _ _ _ _ _ _ _ is it going?
m. Very _ _ _ _ _ _ _, thank you.
n. I'm very _ _ _ _ _ _ _ to see you.
o. Hello Anne, how are _ _ _ _ _ _ _?

**could**
**introduce**
**afternoon**
**how**
**things**
**glad**
**living**
**what**
**well**
**where**
**can**
**meet**
**like**
**occupation**
**good**

## 2. Multiple Choice Wie lautet die korrekte Antwort?

a. *What's your name?*

1. *I am John.*
2. *I am the John.*
3. *I call me John.*

b. *Do you speak English?*

1. *Yes, I can.*
2. *Yes, I do.*
3. *Yes, I speak.*

c. *Where are you from?*

1. *I am being German.*
2. *I am coming from Germany.*
3. *I am from Germany.*

d. *What do you do?*

1. *I am working as a teacher.*
2. *I work as a teacher.*
3. *I do be a teacher.*

e. *Have you ever been to Ireland?*

1. *I was never there.*
2. *I had never been there.*
3. *I have never been there.*

f. *How old are you?*

1. *I am 26 years old.*
2. *I have 26 years.*
3. *I am being 26 years old.*

Lösung 3: GROW: become, cultivate, develop, expand, get bigger, increase FEEL: be aware of, believe, experience, perceive, sense, touch PULL: drag, draw, influence, move, tear, tug STAND: be upright, endure, obtain, place, remain, tolerate

Lösung 2: a. 1 b. 2 c. 3 d. 2 e. 3 f. 1

## 3. Synonyms Ordnen Sie den Verben die richtigen Synonyme zu!

*be aware of, become, believe, be upright, cultivate, develop, drag, draw, endure, experience, expand, get bigger, increase, influence, move, obtain, perceive, place, remain, sense, tear, tolerate, touch, tug*

| GROW: | FEEL: | PULL: | STAND: |
|---|---|---|---|
| ------------ | ------------ | ------------ | ------------ |
| ------------ | ------------ | ------------ | ------------ |
| ------------ | ------------ | ------------ | ------------ |
| ------------ | ------------ | ------------ | ------------ |
| ------------ | ------------ | ------------ | ------------ |
| ------------ | ------------ | ------------ | ------------ |

## 4. NICE TO BE NICE Welche Wörter bedeuten das Gleiche?

| | |
|---|---|
| a. lead | ___ nasty |
| b. stage | ___ glad |
| c. very | ___ certain |
| d. great | ___ result |
| e. effect | ___ beneath |
| f. inquire | ___ affection |
| g. pretty | ___ attempt |
| h. sure | ___ sketch |
| i. under | ___ male |
| j. love | ___ guide |
| k. man | ___ extremely |
| l. draw | ___ phase |
| m. try | ___ big |
| n. bad | ___ ask |
| o. happy | ___ good-looking |

Lösung 5: bar, armchair, bookshelf, desk, sofa, mirror, wardrobe, lamp, TV, bed, clock, table, carpet

Lösung 4: a. lead & guide b. stage & phase c. very & extremely d. great & big e. effect & result f. inquire & ask g. pretty & good-looking h. sure & certain i. under & beneath j. love & affection k. man & male l. draw & sketch m. try & attempt n. bad & nasty o. happy & glad

## 5. FURNITURE Finden Sie die 13 versteckten Möbelstücke!

| | | | | | | | | | | | |
|---|---|---|---|---|---|---|---|---|---|---|---|
| K | C | O | L | C | L | O | C | H | T | L | I |
| I | B | A | R | M | C | H | A | I | R | P | M |
| E | B | O | R | D | R | A | W | F | O | R | I |
| R | L | A | M | P | Q | D | Y | E | O | P | R |
| L | W | A | R | D | E | S | K | N | Y | S | R |
| B | N | T | E | B | V | T | A | B | L | E | O |
| M | O | F | L | E | H | S | K | O | O | B | R |

## 6. Agree & Disagree Was antworten Sie?

| | | | |
|---|---|---|---|
| a. | *I don't like waiting.* | *(agree)* | *Don't you? Neither do I.* |
| b. | *I'd like to go for a swim.* | *(disagree)* | *Would you? I wouldn't.* |
| c. | *I often drink tea.* | *(disagree)* | ______________. |
| d. | *I can't speak Spanish.* | *(agree)* | ______________. |
| e. | *My sister went to school in Wigan.* | *(agree)* | ______________. |
| f. | *We have never been here before.* | *(disagree)* | ______________. |
| g. | *I don't have any change.* | *(disagree)* | ______________. |
| h. | *I didn't enjoy this trip.* | *(agree)* | ______________. |
| i. | *He is afraid of snakes.* | *(agree)* | ______________. |
| j. | *I think I'll go to sleep now.* | *(disagree)* | ______________. |
| k. | *Carol is going to an English course now.* | *(agree)* | ______________. |
| l. | *I wouldn't like to stay in a hotel.* | *(disagree)* | ______________. |
| m. | *I think it's going to rain.* | *(disagree)* | ______________. |
| n. | *I'm looking forward to seeing this film.* | *(agree)* | ______________. |
| o. | *I'd love to stay here forever.* | *(agree)* | ______________. |

Lösung 7: a. grandmother b. uncle c. sister-in-law d. grandchildren e. nephew f. fiancee g. great-grandparents h. niece i. brother j. aunt k. mother-in-law l. cousins m. bride & groom n. husband o. sister

Lösung 6: c. Do you? I don't. d. Can you not? Nor/Neither can I. e. Did she? So did my sister/I. f. Have you not? I/We have. g. Do you not? I do. h. Did you not? Nor/Neither did I. i. Is he? So am I. j. Will you? I won't. k. Is she? So am I. l. Would you not? I would. m. Do you? I don't. n. Are you? So am I. o. Would you? So would I.

## 7. WE ARE FAMILY Wer ist gemeint?

| | | | |
|---|---|---|---|
| a. | *She is your mother's mother.* | | *uncle* |
| b. | *He is your father's brother.* | | *great-grandparents* |
| c. | *She is your brother's wife.* | | *grandmother* |
| d. | *They are your daughter's children.* | | *aunt* |
| e. | *He is your sister's son.* | | *sister-in-law* |
| f. | *She is the person you are going to marry.* | | *husband* |
| g. | *They are your father's grandparents.* | | *brother* |
| h. | *She is your brother's daughter.* | | *fiancee* |
| i. | *He is your parent's son.* | | *sister* |
| j. | *She is your mother's sister.* | | *grandchildren* |
| k. | *She is your husband's mother.* | | *cousins* |
| l. | *They are your uncle's children.* | | *bride & groom* |
| m. | *They stand in front of the altar together.* | | *nephew* |
| n. | *He is the man you married.* | | *niece* |
| o. | *She is your parent's daughter.* | | *mother-in-law* |

## 8. THE ODD ONE OUT Welches Wort passt nicht zu den anderen?

*a. perhaps, possibly, maybe, definitely*

*b. nice, pleasant, kind, rude*

*c. happy, curious, merry, glad*

*d. advanced, modern, distinct, contemporary*

*e. cold, chilly, cool, exciting*

*f. rich, healthy, well-off, wealthy*

*g. little, cute, diminutive, tiny*

*h. shrewd, short, brief, scant*

*i. easy, simple, lazy, effortless*

*j. soft, bright, smooth, mild*

*k. mean, lazy, nasty, foul*

*l. near, closed, beside, adjoining*

*m. often, frequently, ever, regularly*

*n. secret, private, confidential, public*

*o. usual, ambiguous, indefinite, uncertain*

Lösung 9: a. pilot b. postman c. baker d. musician e. author f. architect g. chef h. actor i. policeman j. barber k. barmaid l. mechanic m. judge n. operator o. fireman

Lösung 8: a. definitely b. rude c. curious d. distinct e. exciting f. healthy g. cute h. shrewd i. lazy j. bright k. lazy l. closed m. ever n. public o. usual

## 9. Work it out! Wie heißen diese Berufe?

a. *She flies a plane.* → __________
b. *He delivers letters.* → __________
c. *He makes cakes and bread.* → __________
d. *She makes music for a living.* → __________
e. *She writes books.* → __________
f. *She designs buildings.* → __________
g. *He prepares meals in a restaurant.* → __________
h. *She performs on a stage.* → __________
i. *He maintains order and upholds the law.* → __________
j. *He shaves beards and cuts hair.* → __________
k. *She works behind a bar.* → __________
l. *He repairs your car.* → __________
m. *She can sentence you to jail.* → __________
n. *She connects you to the right phone number.* → __________
o. *He is called when something is burning.* → __________

## 10. Better – Faster – Higher! Wie lautet der Komparativ?

*a. I feel much (good) _ _ _ _ _ _ today!*
*b. They got up (early) _ _ _ _ _ _ than usual.*
*c. I guess we were (lucky) _ _ _ _ _ _ than you.*
*d. This sofa is (comfortable) _ _ _ _ _ _ than the other.*
*e. But it is also (expensive) _ _ _ _ _ _ .*
*f. We could have gotten here much (quick) _ _ _ _ _ _.*
*g. You are (patient) _ _ _ _ _ _ than me.*
*h. You should have taken this cold (serious) _ _ _ _ _ _!*
*i. I thought you were (reliable) _ _ _ _ _ _.*
*j. It's much (cheap) _ _ _ _ _ _ in this supermarket.*
*k. It's (far) _ _ _ _ _ _ away than I thought.*
*l. I think my headache is getting (bad) _ _ _ _ _ _.*
*m. Health and happiness are (important) _ _ _ _ _ _ than money.*
*n. I think you could have done (well) _ _ _ _ _ _.*
*o. They have (much) _ _ _ _ _ _ money than they can ever spend.*

Lösung 11: a. six o'clock p.m./in the evening b. half (past) five a.m./in the morning c. a quarter past four p.m./in the afternoon d. ten to nine a.m./in the morning e. ten to twelve a.m/at midnight f. twelve p.m./at noon g. twenty five past seven a.m./in the morning h. 6:30 i. 14.00 j. 17:00 (am Bahnhof, Flughafen in den USA) k. 21:50 l. 11:30 m. 14:45 n. 0:00 o. 17.15

Lösung 10: a. better b. earlier c. luckier d. more comfortable e. more expensive f. quicker g. more patient h. more seriously i. more reliable j. cheaper k. further l. worse m. more important n. better o. more

## 11. Time is ticking away Formen Sie die Uhrzeit in Worte bzw. Zahlen um!

| | | |
|---|---|---|
| *a.* | *18:00* | ________________ |
| *b.* | *5:30* | ________________ |
| *c.* | *16:15* | ________________ |
| *d.* | *8:50* | ________________ |
| *e.* | *23:55* | ________________ |
| *f.* | *12.00* | ________________ |
| *g.* | *7.25* | ________________ |
| *h.* | *half past six in the morning* | ________________ |
| *i.* | *two o'clock in the afternoon* | ________________ |
| *j.* | *seventeen hundred* | ________________ |
| *k.* | *twenty to ten at night* | ________________ |
| *l.* | *eleven thirty a.m.* | ________________ |
| *m.* | *a quarter to three p.m.* | ________________ |
| *n.* | *exactly at midnight* | ________________ |
| *o.* | *a quarter past five p.m.* | ________________ |

## 12. HAPPY DAYS Wie lauten die Superlative?

a. *What was the (enjoyable) ___________ holiday you ever had?*
b. *The (good) ___________ one must have been last year's.*
c. *We stayed in the (cheap) ___________ hotel in town.*
d. *But we had the (nice) ___________ room in the hotel.*
e. *We had the (delicious) ___________ meals.*
f. *We climbed the (high) ___________ mountains.*
g. *We visited the (old) ___________ churches.*
h. *We saw the (valuable) ___________ painting in the world.*
i. *The (hot) ___________ day we spent on the beach.*
j. *In the evening I had the (bad) ___________ sunburn!*
k. *And we met the (lovely) ___________ people there.*
l. *I had the (interesting) ___________ talk with this professor from Harvard.*
m. *He must be the (intelligent) ___________ man I ever met.*
n. *And he was the (generous) ___________ man, too.*
o. *It must have been the (happy) ___________ time of my life!*

Lösung 13: a. the fourteenth of February nineteen ninety nine b. December first nineteen eighty four c. sixteen hundred Dollars/one thousand six hundred Dollars d. seven Dollars twenty five (cents) e. eleven thousand five hundred and sixty five pounds f. fifty pence g. nine fifteen in the evening h. eighty four point five per cent i. half a pint j. seventy three yards k. one ounce l. six feet two inches m. four hundred and twenty seven miles n. fifteen stone o. twelve inches

Lösung 12: a. most enjoyable b. best c. cheapest d. nicest e. most delicious f. highest g. oldest h. most valuable i. hottest j. worst k. loveliest l. most interesting m. most intelligent n. most generous o. happiest

## 13. Numbers, Numbers, Numbers Wie heißt es in Worten?

a. *14/02/1999* ____________________
b. *Dec 1st, 1984* ____________________
c. *$ 1,600* ____________________
d. *$ 7.25* ____________________
e. *£ 11,565* ____________________
f. *50 p* ____________________
g. *9.15 p.m.* ____________________
h. *84,5 %* ____________________
i. *1/2 pt.* ____________________
j. *73 yds.* ____________________
k. *1 oz.* ____________________
l. *6 ft. 2 in.* ____________________
m. *427 mi.* ____________________
n. *15 st.* ____________________
o. *12"* ____________________

## 14. Work it out! Wo arbeiten diese Leute?

| | |
|---|---|
| a. pilot | ___ kitchen |
| b. policeman | ___ bank |
| c. butcher | ___ victuallers |
| d. librarian | ___ airplane |
| e. clown | ___ hospital |
| f. miner | ___ convent |
| g. baker | ___ circus |
| h. surgeon | ___ bakery |
| i. chef | ___ police station |
| j. teller | ___ pharmacy |
| k. pharmacist | ___ post office |
| l. postman | ___ library |
| m. teacher | ___ restaurant |
| n. nun | ___ mine |
| o. waitress | ___ school |

Lösung 15: a. rebuild b. restart c. rewinding d. reload e. reuse f. readmission g. refill h. reset i. rephrase j. reheat k. reopen l. redirected m. rearrange n. rerouted o. rescheduled

Lösung 14: a. airplane b. policestation c. victuallers d. library e. circus f. mine g. bakery h. hospital i. kitchen j. bank k. pharmacy l. post office m. school n. convent o. restaurant

## 15. THE PREFIX "RE-" Was passt in die Lücken?

a. *After the fire I decided to _____ the summer house.*
b. *Johns computer crashed so he had to _____ it.*
c. *You have to pay a fine if you return a video without _____ it.*
d. *My computer caught a virus so I had to _____ all the software.*
e. *We're trying to protect the environment so we _____ all of our glass jars.*
f. *Sorry there's no _____ to the concert once you leave.*
g. *How much is a _____ for this fountain pen?*
h. *There was a power-cut so I had to _____ the video recorder.*
i. *I don't understand, could you _____ that?*
j. *Kevin decided to _____ some stew instead of ordering a pizza delivery.*
k. *The museum is closed now but will _____ on Monday morning.*
l. *We were quite lost but a helpful policewoman _____ us towards the city centre.*
m. *When the baby is born they'll have to _____ their house.*
n. *There were roadworks and traffic was _____.*
o. *I'm afraid the weather is so bad that our sailing has been _____.*

**refill**
**rewinding**
**rearrange**
**reopen**
**rephrase**
**reuse**
**restart**
**redirected**
**reset**
**rebuild**
**readmission**
**reload**
**reheat**
**rescheduled**
**rerouted**

## 16. PARTS OF THE BODY Finden Sie die 17 versteckten Körperteile!

| | | | | | | | | | | | |
|---|---|---|---|---|---|---|---|---|---|---|---|
| D | N | A | H | A | I | R | K | C | A | B | R |
| A | F | O | O | L | E | G | P | A | Q | M | D |
| C | H | I | N | W | A | I | S | T | O | R | B |
| H | E | O | N | E | C | K | T | U | O | A | F |
| S | S | A | E | G | Y | C | T | O | M | E | G |
| E | Y | E | D | A | E | H | O | S | O | L | I |
| C | H | E | S | T | R | R | S | R | E | F | P |

Lösung 17: a. any b. any c. some d. any e. any f. some g. any h. some
i. any j. some k. any l. any m. some n. some o. any

Lösung 16: hair, eye, nose, mouth, ear, chin, neck, head, chest, back, arm, hand, finger, waist, leg, foot, toe

## 17. Any which way Setzen Sie "some" oder "any" ein!

a. *Are there _________ football clubs in this town?*
b. *Have you got _________ change for the cigarette machine?*
c. *I have _________ very rare pieces of vinyl that you might like.*
d. *I don't have _________ local money just American dollars.*
e. *Why aren't there _________ buses after six o'clock on Saturdays?*
f. *Have you enough money to get _________ French fries on the way home?*
g. *They don't seem to have _________ buses going near our hotel.*
h. *Come over here, I have _________ friends I would like you to meet.*
i. *I asked our landlady if she could get us _________ tickets for the concert tonight.*
j. *_________ of us will have to wait and get a second taxi.*
k. *Are there _________ other places of historical interest for us to visit?*
l. *It's a long time since I got _________ help with the gardening.*
m. *It's good fun in this bar but we'd rather have _________ seats.*
n. *The manager has just gone to organise _________ alternative accomodation.*
o. *I had an awful headache but couldn't find _________ aspirin.*

## 18. "UNDER THE WEATHER" Füllen Sie die Lücken!

*Tony: I've got a splitting headache. Would you have (a) _ _ _ _ _ _ _ _ I can take to clear it up?*

*Amanda: Sure. Here's an apirin and I'm sure that you'd like (b) _ _ _ _ _ _ _ _ to wash it down with. Unfortunately (c) _ _ _ _ _ _ _ _ has drank all the bottled water. Do you mind drinking tap water?*

*Tony: No. Not at all. I'll drink anything! I think what I really need to do is lie down (d) _ _ _ _ _ _ _ _.*

*Amanda: Yes, you do look quite tired. When you've drunk that you could go and lie down in the guest bedroom. It's quiet and there won't be (e)_ _ _ _ _ _ _ _ to bother you.*

*Tony: Thanks. I don't want to put (f)_ _ _ _ _ _ _ _ out I would have slept (g) _ _ _ _ _ _ _ _!*

*Amanda: Don't mention it. I have to go to work now so I'll see you (h) _ _ _ _ _ _ _ _ tonight. Don't worry about the cat, (i) _ _ _ _ _ _ _ _ will feed him later.*

*Tony: Okay. Thanks again.*

*Amanda: (j) _ _ _ _ _ _ _ _!*

Lösung 19: GIVE: deliver, donate, hand over, present, provide, supply GET: achieve, acquire, attain, capture, receive, win MAKE: build, construct, create, fabricate, form, produce HAVE: hold, keep, obtain, own, possess, retain

Lösung 18: a. anything b. something c. somebody d. somewhere e. anybody f. anyone g. anywhere h. sometime i. someone j. anytime

## 19. Synonyms Ordnen Sie den Verben die richtigen Synonyme zu!

*achieve, acquire, attain, build, capture, construct, create, deliver, donate, fabricate, form, hand over, hold, keep, obtain, own, possess, present, produce, provide, receive, retain, supply, win*

| GIVE: | GET: | MAKE: | HAVE: |
| --- | --- | --- | --- |
| ------------------ | ------------------ | ------------------ | ------------------ |
| ------------------ | ------------------ | ------------------ | ------------------ |
| ------------------ | ------------------ | ------------------ | ------------------ |
| ------------------ | ------------------ | ------------------ | ------------------ |
| ------------------ | ------------------ | ------------------ | ------------------ |
| ------------------ | ------------------ | ------------------ | ------------------ |

## 20. COMPOUNDING THE FACT Wie kann man das Folgende einfacher ausdrücken?

a. a room on the second floor ______
b. a hike that takes five days ______
c. a bottle that holds two litres ______
d. a journey of twenty miles ______
e. a dinner lit with candles ______
f. a cart drawn by a horse ______
g. a race with three legs ______
h. a girl with brown eyes ______
i. a man born in Dublin ______
j. a hotel with four stars ______
k. a book that has 800 pages ______
l. a child that is nine years old ______
m. an apartment with one bedroom ______
n. a gentleman with an odd look ______
o. a woman with long hair ______

Lösung 21: SHOW: display, prove, reveal, demonstrate, present PUT: place, deposit, lay, rest, position, set SEE: meet, check, read, notice, visit, imagine SAY: mention, remark, announce, tell, answer, convey, express

Lösung 20: a. a second-floor room b. a five-day hike c. a two-litre bottle d. a twenty-mile journey e. a candle-lit dinner f. a horse-drawn cart g. a three-legged race h. a brown-eyed girl i. a Dublin-born man j. a four-star hotel k. an 800-page book l. a nine-year-old child m. a one-bedroomed apartment n. an odd-looking gentleman o. a long-haired woman

## 21. Synonyms Ordnen Sie den Verben die richtigen Synonyme zu!

*place, display, meet, mention, express, rest, reveal, set, imagine, convey, answer, position, tell, deposit, check, visit, present, announce, read, demonstrate, notice, lay, prove, remark*

| SHOW: | PUT: | SEE: | SAY: |
| --- | --- | --- | --- |
| ------------------ | ------------------ | ------------------ | ------------------ |
| ------------------ | ------------------ | ------------------ | ------------------ |
| ------------------ | ------------------ | ------------------ | ------------------ |
| ------------------ | ------------------ | ------------------ | ------------------ |
| ------------------ | ------------------ | ------------------ | ------------------ |
| ------------------ | ------------------ | ------------------ | ------------------ |

## 22. THE OTHER SIDE OF THE TRACKS Welche Gegenteile gehören zusammen?

| | |
|---|---|
| a. circular | ___ advance |
| b. risky | ___ build |
| c. disappointed | ___ public |
| d. long winded | ___ routine |
| e. inclusive | ___ succinct |
| f. restricted | ___ delighted |
| g. flexible | ___ certain |
| h. contaminated | ___ square |
| i. lowly | ___ elevated |
| j. halt | ___ pure |
| k. minor | ___ major |
| l. extraordinary | ___ stiff |
| m. secret | ___ continue |
| n. demolish | ___ open |
| o. retreat | ___ excluded |

Lösung 23: a. until b. as soon as c. once d. while e. now f. whenever g. not until h. now i. as soon as j. once k. until l. not until m. whenever n. while

Lösung 22: a. circular & square b. risky & certain c. disappointed & delighted d. long winded & succinct e. inclusive & excluded f. restricted & open g. flexible & stiff h. contaminated & pure i. lowly & elevated j. halt & continue k. minor & major l. extraordinary & routine m. secret & public n. demolish & build o. retreat & advance

## 23. Time is on your side Setzen Sie die richtigen Wörter ein!

| | | |
|---|---|---|
| a. | *Martin stayed _ _ _ _ the end of the concert and got to see the encore.* | **until** |
| b. | *It started to rain _ _ _ _ we arrived at the beach.* | **once** |
| c. | *_ _ _ _ we have the tent erected, we can start to cook.* | **as soon as** |
| d. | *Okay, you put up the tent _ _ _ _ I open a tin of beans.* | **whenever** |
| e. | *Dinner will be served at six o'clock and it's 17:45 _ _ _ _.* | **not until** |
| f. | *_ _ _ _ I'm hungry and too tired to cook I like to order a pizza delivery.* | **now** |
| g. | *It was _ _ _ _ the film was over did I realise that it was in black and white!* | **while** |
| h. | *_ _ _ _ and again we go out to dinner with friends.* | **whenever** |
| i. | *_ _ _ _ the car is fixed we can drive down to Clifden to visit the festival.* | **until** |
| j. | *Kelly had a dalmatian _ _ _ _ that won several competitions.* | **not until** |
| k. | *We have to wait _ _ _ _ Monday morning for the next flight out of Crete.* | **while** |
| l. | *You can enter with an official ticket and _ _ _ _ then.* | **as soon as** |
| m. | *Gareth stays in my house _ _ _ _ he visits London.* | **once** |
| n. | *My mother arranged a surprise birthday party _ _ _ _ I was in work.* | **now** |

## 24. Mixed and Matched Welche Wörter bedeuten das Gleiche?

| | |
|---|---|
| a. same | gather |
| b. tame | clash |
| c. evil | preserve |
| d. miss | between |
| e. open | overlook |
| f. pin | sleep |
| g. exit | alike |
| h. collect | apply |
| i. among | free |
| j. collide | docile |
| k. active | doing |
| l. keep | door |
| m. rest | bad |
| n. use | attach |

Lösung 25: a. What's your name? b. Where are you from? c. What do you do (for a living)? d. How are you? e. How old are you? f. Are you married? g. Have you been to/visited Germany before?

Lösung 24: a. same & alike b. tame & docile c. evil & bad d. miss & overlook e. open & free f. pin & attach g. exit & door h. collect & gather i. among & between j. collide & clash k. active & doing l. keep & preserve m. rest & sleep n. use & apply

## 25. ASK THE QUESTION! Stellen Sie die entsprechende Frage für jede Antwort!

a. ___________________________________________?
*My name is Caroline.*

b. ___________________________________________?
*I'm from Newcastle.*

c. ___________________________________________?
*I'm a teacher.*

d. ___________________________________________?
*I'm fine, thanks.*

e. ___________________________________________?
*I'm twenty nine years old.*

f. ___________________________________________?
*No, I'm single.*

g. ___________________________________________?
*No, this is my first visit to Germany.*

## 26. QUESTIONS Setzen Sie das richtige Fragewort ein!

a. ______ *is your phone number?*
b. ______ *is this hat?*
c. ______ *will you be coming to see us?*
d. ______ *books do you prefer in general?*
e. ______ *did you get these flowers from?*
f. ______ *is the weather like?*
g. ______ *much is that?*
h. ______ *did you go last night?*
i. ______ *of you said they wanted more homework?*
j. ______ *many were at the meeting?*
k. ______ *shall I invite to the party?*
l. ______ *did you talk about with him?*
m. ______ *one do you prefer?*
n. ______ *do you think so?*
o. ______ *way is the right one?*

Lösung 27: a. unexpected b. non-alcoholic c. disconnected d. immature e. unpack f. impossible g. misinterpreted h. immoral i. disappeared j. inflexible k. irregular l. illegitimate m. irresistible n. decentralized o. non-smoking

Lösung 26: a. What b. Whose c. When d. Which e. Who f. What g. How h. Where i. Who j. How k. Who l. What m. Which n. Why o. Which

## 27. Negative Prefixes Welche Vorsilbe macht das Wort negativ?

| | | |
|---|---|---|
| a. | *This came to me really _ _ _ _expectedly!* | **un-** |
| b. | *We only serve _ _ _ _alcoholic drinks here.* | **in-** |
| c. | *Our phone was _ _ _ _connected because we didn't pay the bill.* | **im-** |
| d. | *He is very _ _ _ _mature for his age.* | **dis-** |
| e. | *We didn't even have time to _ _ _ _pack our suitcases.* | **non-** |
| f. | *This is absolutely _ _ _ _possible.* | **il-** |
| g. | *She completely _ _ _ _interpreted the whole situation.* | **mis-** |
| h. | *It would be very _ _ _ _moral to do such a thing.* | **ir-** |
| i. | *He _ _ _ _appeared without a trace.* | **un-** |
| j. | *Don't be so _ _ _ _flexible!* | **dis-** |
| k. | *I will never remember all the _ _ _ _regular verbs.* | **im-** |
| l. | *I did not know he had an _ _ _ _legitimate daughter.* | **de-** |
| m. | *This guy thinks he's _ _ _ _resistible.* | **ir-** |
| n. | *They _ _ _ _ centralized their whole production.* | **non-** |
| o. | *I'd rather sit in the _ _ _ _smoking section.* | **im-** |

## 28. More Prefixes Setzen Sie die passenden Vorsilben ein!

| | | |
|---|---|---|
| a. | *This was an _ _ _ _ standing performance!* | **over-** |
| b. | *Sorry, that I´m late this morning, but I _ _ _ _slept.* | **out-** |
| c. | *Excuse me, I think you _ _ _ _charged me.* | **super-** |
| d. | *This politician is _ _ _ _conservative.* | **hyper-** |
| e. | *It must have been a _ _ _ _natural phenomenon.* | **ultra-** |
| f. | *Be careful, she´s _ _ _ _sensitive.* | **hyper-** |
| g. | *I think you´re _ _ _ _critical of this.* | **over-** |
| h. | *I don´t like those _ _ _ _modern paintings.* | **cut-** |
| i. | *She´s an _ _ _ _ pretective mother.* | **over-** |
| j. | *Maybe it´s because she´s got a _ _ _ _active child.* | **over-** |
| k. | *He _ _ _ _ lived all his brothers and sisters.* | **out-** |
| l. | *I _ _ _ _drew my bank account again.* | **over-** |
| m. | *She is such a good athlete, she _ _ _ _classes all the others.* | **super-** |
| n. | *If you _ _ _ _cook your vegetables they loose a lot of vitamins.* | **ultra-** |
| o. | *Batman is a _ _ _ _hero.* | **over-** |

Lösung 29: a. when b. which c. who d. which e. who f. which g. who h. who i. who j. when k. where l. which m. when n. which o. when

Lösung 28: a. outstanding b. overslept c. overcharged d. ultra-conservative e. supernatural f. hypersensitive g. overcritical h. ultra-modern i. overprotective j. hyperactive k. outlived l. overdrew m. outclasses n. overcook o. superhero

## 29. Childhood Memories Wie muss es heißen?

| | |
|---|---|
| a. *Do you want to see a picture of ____ I was a child?* | **which** |
| b. *This is a photograph of the primary ____ I went to.* | **who** |
| c. *And here's a picture of everyone ____ was in my class.* | **when** |
| d. *School uniforms are something ____ is typical for British schools.* | **where** |
| e. *Look, this is the boy ____ I sat next to for all the years.* | **who** |
| f. *He always made jokes ____ everybody thought were hilarious.* | **when** |
| g. *But he was also the one ____ always knew the right answers.* | **which** |
| h. *Mr. Jones, our maths teacher was the one ____ I liked best.* | **which** |
| i. *He was also the headmaster, the person ____ directed the school.* | **when** |
| j. *Twelve o'clock was the time ____ we had our lunchbreak.* | **who** |
| k. *There was a cafeteria ____ we got our food.* | **who** |
| l. *Monday was the day ____ I always liked best.* | **when** |
| m. *Because Monday afternoon was the time ____ we had physical education.* | **which** |
| n. *I didn't really like the ball games ____ we were playing.* | **which** |
| o. *But I loved it ____ we went swimming.* | **who** |

## 30. BREAKFAST OF CHAMPIONS Setzen Sie die richtigen Wörter ein!

*When I was a boy every Sunday my mother made us a traditional (a)______. She filled the frying pan with cooking (b)______ and heated it slowly. The next step was to throw in the (c)______, the essential part of a large fry! Then she would cook the (d)_____ ____ which we also called (e)______. My father always liked some (f)________ mushrooms with his breakfast. My mother also used to cook black and white (g)_______, which nobody really liked. We children preferred baked (h) _______ with our breakfast. Finally, my mother would cook us some (i)_______. Everybody liked their eggs differently in our house, but I liked (j) _______ eggs best. With our breakfast we had buttered (k) ___________ and a glass of (l) ______ ______. My sister didn't like big breakfasts, she only had a bowl of (m) _________ with milk. Our breakfast of champions was always finished with a nice pot of (n)________.*

**eggs**
**scrambled**
**rashers**
**tea**
**fry**
**beans**
**oil**
**sausages**
**streaky bacon**
**fried**
**pudding**
**cereals**
**orange juice**
**toast**

Lösung 31: APPLY: use, put on, be valid, exercise, employ, paint REALIZE: understand, notice, discover, achieve, recognize, fulfill FINISH: end, stop, cease, conclude, ruin, close CUT: slice, reduce, lower, mow, shorten, chop

Lösung 30: a. fry b. oil c. sausages d. streaky bacon e. rashers f. fried g. pudding h. beans i. eggs j. scrambled k. toast l. orange juice m. cereals n. tea

## 31. SYNONYMS Ordnen Sie den Verben die richtigen Synonyme zu!

*put on, close, reduce, achieve, employ, ruin, lower, exercise, cease, use, mow, recognize, be valid, shorten, stop, discover, chop, paint, end, notice, slice, conclude, understand, fulfill*

| APPLY: | REALIZE: | FINISH: | CUT: |
| --- | --- | --- | --- |
| ------------------ | ------------------ | ------------------ | ------------------ |
| ------------------ | ------------------ | ------------------ | ------------------ |
| ------------------ | ------------------ | ------------------ | ------------------ |
| ------------------ | ------------------ | ------------------ | ------------------ |
| ------------------ | ------------------ | ------------------ | ------------------ |
| ------------------ | ------------------ | ------------------ | ------------------ |

## 32. Mixed and Matched Finden Sie die Synonyme!

| | |
|---|---|
| a. often | normal |
| b. pupil | reality |
| c. edge | frequently |
| d. old | modern |
| e. quality | drop |
| f. custom | habit |
| g. new | elderly |
| h. fall | student |
| i. problem | plump |
| j. break | bold |
| k. usual | property |
| l. fat | smash |
| m. brave | border |
| n. fact | worry |
| o. alike | similar |

Lösung 33: a. gentle & tender b. ugly & nasty c. area & region d. crash & accident e. number & figure f. cause & reason g. tight & mean h. power & energy i. keep & save j. zero & nought k. tube & pipe l. hat & cap m. bag & sack n. pay & wages o. bet & wager

Lösung 32: a. often & frequently b. pupil & student c. edge & border d. old & elderly e. quality & property f. custom & habit g. new & modern h. fall & drop i. problem & worry j. break & smash k. usual & normal l. fat & plump m. brave & bold n. fact & reality o. alike & similar

## 33. Mixed and Matched Welche Wörter bedeuten dasselbe?

| | |
|---|---|
| a. gentle | reason |
| b. ugly | cap |
| c. area | nought |
| d. crash | tender |
| e. number | energy |
| f. cause | mean |
| g. tight | save |
| h. power | pipe |
| i. keep | sack |
| j. zero | region |
| k. tube | wages |
| l. hat | accident |
| m. bag | figure |
| n. pay | nasty |
| o. bet | wager |

## 34. Don't confuse! Streichen Sie das falsche Wort durch!

a. *Our gas heating is very* ***economic/economical****.*
b. *The signing of the Magna Carta was an* ***historic/historical*** *event.*
c. *Our daughter is studying to become an* ***electric/electrical*** *engineer.*
d. *We have a wide selection of* ***classic/classical*** *music among our CD collection.*
e. *These documents are of great* ***historic/historical*** *importance.*
f. *No* ***alcoholic/alcoholical*** *drinks are served on this flight.*
g. *This sentence is grammatically incorrect, but that's* ***poetic/poetical*** *license.*
h. *Let me ask you a* ***theoretic/theoretical*** *question.*
i. *We had an* ***electric/electrical*** *heating system installed last month.*
j. *That was a* ***classic/classical*** *example of English understatement.*
k. *This country is heading towards an* ***economic/economical*** *crisis.*
l. *He's so* ***pessimistic/pessimistical*** *about everything.*
m. *Saving the child was so* ***heroic/heroical*** *of him.*
n. *I had to do a* ***psychologic/psychological*** *test in the interview.*
o. *They are trying to improve the* ***public/publical*** *transport system.*

Lösung 35: TIE: bind, fasten, link, connect, join, draw LOOK: glance, peek, stare, seem, appear, gaze GROW: increase, become, cultivate, expand, swell, develop CRY: weep, bawl, scream, shout, blubber, sob

Lösung 34: a. economical b. historic c. electrical d. classical e. historical f. alcoholic g. poetic h. theoretical i. electric j. classic k. economic l. pessimistic m. heroic n. psycholigical o. public

## 35. SYNONYMS Ordnen Sie den Verben die richtigen Synonyme zu!

*seem, cultivate, link, stare, scream, expand, appear, join, become, bawl, fasten, develop, gaze, connect, glance, blubber, peek, bind, swell, increase, weep, draw, shout, sob*

| TIE: | LOOK: | GROW: | CRY: |
| --- | --- | --- | --- |
| ------------------ | ------------------ | ------------------ | ------------------ |
| ------------------ | ------------------ | ------------------ | ------------------ |
| ------------------ | ------------------ | ------------------ | ------------------ |
| ------------------ | ------------------ | ------------------ | ------------------ |
| ------------------ | ------------------ | ------------------ | ------------------ |
| ------------------ | ------------------ | ------------------ | ------------------ |

## 36. Match the Opposites! Welche Wörter bedeuten das Gegenteil?

| | |
|---|---|
| a. *intact* | *simple* |
| b. *dark* | *lost* |
| c. *owner* | *brief* |
| d. *certain* | *common* |
| e. *difficult* | *friend* |
| f. *huge* | *different* |
| g. *long* | *bright* |
| h. *silly* | *polite* |
| i. *unique* | *sober* |
| j. *hobby* | *damaged* |
| k. *enemy* | *career* |
| l. *found* | *tenant* |
| m. *identical* | *minute* |
| n. *rude* | *unsure* |
| o. *hairy* | *bald* |

Lösung 37: a. joy b. crochet c. shirk d. class e. thick f. quirky g. groove h. covet i. tardy j. shunt k. malign l. gorge m. aural n. grade o. leave

Lösung 36: a. intact & damaged b. dark & bright c. owner & tenant d. certain & unsure e. difficult & simple f. huge & minute g. long & brief h. silly & sober i. unique & common j. hobby & career k. enemy & friend l. found & lost m. identical & different n. rude & polite o. hairy & bald

## 37. ODD ONE OUT! Finden Sie das schwarze Schaf!

a. *rheumatism, flu, angina, joy*

b. *crochet, skiing, polo, cricket*

c. *shock, fright, shirk, scare*

d. *bright, class, smart, clever*

e. *slim, lean, thick, thin*

f. *quirky, quiet, calm, silent*

g. *grab, grope, grasp, groove*

h. *long, covet, lengthy, extended*

i. *normal, average, tardy, typical*

j. *shunt, aid, sense, assist*

k. *dirty, malign, muddy, messy*

l. *gorge, aim, goal, purpose*

m. *oral, verbal, spoken, aural*

n. *grade, flat, even, level*

o. *rent, let, leave, hire*

## 38. One or the Other Streichen Sie das richtige Wort an!

a. *Seven people is a big family and a lot of mouths to* ***feet/feed****.*
b. *I'm afraid that the hotel looks like a building* ***side/site****.*
c. *I'm not quite sure* ***where/were*** *Charles has gone to see the hockey match.*
d. *I'm sure that the hotel has a* ***save/safe*** *where you can put the jewels.*
e. *The last time I went on holidays to Majorca I didn't even get a* ***ten/tan****.*
f. *I think he said that the cheque was in the* ***mail/male****.*
g. *It was eerie how* ***quiet/quite*** *everything became before the storm broke.*
h. *I believe he was flying by the* ***seed/seat*** *of his pants!*
i. *That offence carries a mandatory* ***life/live*** *sentence in that country.*
j. *It appears that Kirsty has changed her* ***stile/style*** *of dress again.*
k. *Joey thought that the special* ***affects/effects*** *were the most realistic so far.*
l. *I'm sure that wasn't the smell of her* ***feat/feet.***
m. *Everybody in the pub* ***sighed/side*** *when Celbridge United lost the final match.*
n. *I really think that you should* ***were/wear*** *your blue dress to the graduation.*

Lösung 39: coat, dress, hat, jacket, shirt, shoes, skirt, socks, trousers, tie, vest, underpants.

Lösung 38: a. feed b. site c. where d. safe e. tan f. mail g. quiet h. seat i. life j. style k. effects l. feet m. sighed n. wear

## 39. The Latest Fashion

Finden Sie die 12 versteckten Kleidungsstücke!

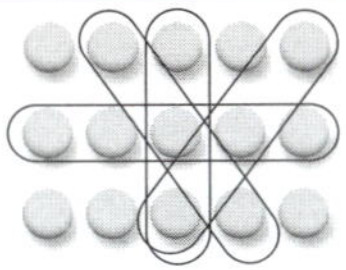

| | | | | | | | | | | | |
|---|---|---|---|---|---|---|---|---|---|---|---|
| S | P | M | J | K | V | E | S | T | L | F | K |
| O | S | E | T | A | O | C | H | R | I | O | L |
| C | E | P | I | R | C | S | K | I | R | T | M |
| K | O | C | E | D | O | K | M | H | A | T | R |
| S | H | P | H | C | D | R | E | S | S | A | I |
| K | S | R | E | S | U | O | R | T | L | M | P |
| E | S | T | N | A | P | R | E | D | N | U | L |

## 40. Silly about Synonyms! Ordnen Sie die richtige Synonyme zu!

| | |
|---|---|
| a. guess | maintenance |
| b. stage | pity |
| c. hit | phase |
| d. motor | business |
| e. precious | valuable |
| f. service | everyday |
| g. sympathy | suppose |
| h. team | situation |
| i. trade | spicy |
| j. usual | success |
| k. wise | property |
| l. case | sensible |
| m. hot | engine |
| n. land | group |

Lösung 41: PICK: choose, select, pluck, elect, open, gather LIE: fib, fabricate, repose, lounge, rest, falsify DRIVE: steer, power, rush, force, push, send TOUCH: feel, grasp, move, contact, style, affect

Lösung 40: a. guess & suppose b. stage & phase c. hit & success d. motor & engine e. precious & valuable f. service & maintenance g. sympathy & pity h. team & group i. trade & business j. usual & everyday k.wise & sensible l. case & situation m. hot & spicy n. land & property

## 41. Synonyms

Ordnen Sie den Verben die richtigen Synonyme zu!

*falsify, open, force, contact, pluck, repose, push, grasp, fib, choose, affect, send, power, select, style, rush, steer, elect, rest, move, gather, fabricate, feel, lounge*

| PICK: | LIE: | DRIVE: | TOUCH: |
|---|---|---|---|
| ____ | ____ | ____ | ____ |
| ____ | ____ | ____ | ____ |
| ____ | ____ | ____ | ____ |
| ____ | ____ | ____ | ____ |
| ____ | ____ | ____ | ____ |
| ____ | ____ | ____ | ____ |

## 42. HOLIDAYS Kennen Sie die Feiertage?

| | |
|---|---|
| a. *On a Bank Holiday...* | 1. *...some people drink green beer.* |
| b. *On Christmas Day...* | 2. *...Americans celebrate their independence.* |
| c. *Boxing Day...* | 3. *...all public services and shops are closed.* |
| d. *On St. Patrick's Day...* | 4. *...good Catholics don't eat meat or drink alcohol.* |
| e. *On Good Friday...* | 5. *...starts in February.* |
| f. *At Easter...* | 6. *...is also known as St. Stephen's Day.* |
| g. *On Thanksgiving Day...* | 7. *...is a feast for Jews.* |
| h. *On the Fourth of July...* | 8. *...the birth of Christ is celebrated.* |
| i. *On Halloween...* | 9. *...Muslims have to fast.* |
| j. *Passover...* | 10. *...is in remembrance of a great civil rights leader.* |
| k. *On Valentine's Day...* | 11. *...you get to eat a lot of eggs.* |
| l. *Pancake Tuesday...* | 12. *...Americans eat a big Turkey.* |
| m. *Martin Luther King Day...* | 13. *...is the day before Ash Wednesday.* |
| n. *The Chinese New Year...* | 14. *...kids get to trick or treat.* |
| o. *At Ramadan...* | 15. *...you give flowers to your sweetheart.* |

Lösung 43: a. flat & apartment b. first floor & second floor c. ground floor & first floor d. lift & elevator e. toilet & bathroom f. wardrobe & closet g. waistcoat & vest h. trousers & pants i. holiday & vacation j. autumn & fall k. rubbish & garbage l. cinema & movie theater m. film & movie n. queue & line o. crisps & chips

Lösung 42: a. 3 b. 8 c. 6 d. 1 e. 4 f. 11 g. 12 h. 2 i. 14 j. 7 k. 15 l. 13 m. 10 n. 5 o. 9

## 43. British & American English Welche Wörter bedeuten das Gleiche?

| | |
|---|---|
| a. *flat* | *bathroom* |
| b. *first floor* | *fall* |
| c. *ground floor* | *second floor* |
| d. *lift* | *garbage* |
| e. *toilet* | *movie theater* |
| f. *wardrobe* | *apartment* |
| g. *waistcoat* | *line* |
| h. *trousers* | *chips* |
| i. *holiday* | *first floor* |
| j. *autumn* | *movie* |
| k. *rubbish* | *elevator* |
| l. *cinema* | *closet* |
| m. *film* | *vest* |
| n. *queue* | *vacation* |
| o. *crisps* | *pants* |

## 44. Surfing the Net Finden Sie zwölf versteckte Computerausdrücke!

| | | | | | | | | | | | |
|---|---|---|---|---|---|---|---|---|---|---|---|
| O | N | L | I | T | E | N | R | E | T | N | I |
| N | F | I | L | B | R | O | W | S | E | R | C |
| L | I | F | B | A | C | K | U | P | Y | M | Y |
| I | L | B | L | A | P | S | U | R | F | O | B |
| N | E | L | E | I | N | T | B | E | W | D | E |
| E | R | D | W | N | L | O | O | D | O | E | R |
| M | I | L | I | A | M | E | M | P | I | M | S |

Lösung 45: a. creditor & debtor b. patient & doctor c. horse & jockey d. superior & subordinate e. employee & employer f. host & guest g. angel & devil h. salesperson & customer i. driver & passenger j. queen & king k. husband & wife l. bride & groom m. master & servant n. predator & prey

Lösung 44: online, email, surf, web, browser, modem, internet, cyber, offline, laptop, backup, file

## 45. Matching Pairs Welche Paare gehören zusammen?

a. creditor
b. patient
c. horse
d. superior
e. employee
f. host
g. angel
h. salesperson
i. driver
j. queen
k. husband
l. bride
m. master
n. predator

&

- prey
- passenger
- king
- servant
- doctor
- groom
- guest
- subordinate
- jockey
- devil
- customer
- debtor
- wife
- employer

## 46. Have a nice Flight! Was/wer ist gemeint?

| | |
|---|---|
| a. *He/she serves the drinks.* | ◯ *duty free* |
| b. *So you can get a good view.* | ◯ *wings* |
| c. *somebody to fly the plane* | ◯ *air sickness* |
| d. *You leave one and arrive in another.* | ◯ *flight attendant* |
| e. *Don't leave home without one.* | ◯ *pilot* |
| f. *You are what you are.* | ◯ *window seat* |
| g. *You can't get on the plane without one.* | ◯ *passport* |
| h. *On long flights you will need some.* | ◯ *boarding pass* |
| i. *If you are unlucky, you will experience this.* | ◯ *airport* |
| j. *The plane won't get far without them.* | ◯ *first class* |
| k. *where the pilot sits when flying* | ◯ *life jacket* |
| l. *You collect it when you disembark.* | ◯ *baggage* |
| m. *goods offered at a discount* | ◯ *cockpit* |
| n. *Hopefully you'll never need one!* | ◯ *inflight entertainment* |
| o. *the best way to fly* | ◯ *passenger* |

Lösung 47: a. motorway & freeway b. railway & railroad c. crossroads & intersection d. estate car & station wagon e. petrol & gas f. pavement & sidewalk g. underground & subway h. city centre & downtown i. torch & flashlight j. timetable & schedule k. solicitor & attorney l. chemist's & drugstore m. tick & checkmark n. tap & faucet o. zip & zipper

Lösung 46: a. flight attendant b. window seat c. pilot d. airport e. passport f. passenger g. boarding pass h. inflight entertainment i. air sickness j. wings k. cockpit l. baggage m. duty free n. life jacket o. first class

## 47. British & American English

Welche Wörter bedeuten dasselbe?

| | |
|---|---|
| a. motorway | ___ station wagon |
| b. railway | ___ gas |
| c. crossroads | ___ subway |
| d. estate car | ___ flashlight |
| e. petrol | ___ schedule |
| f. pavement | ___ checkmark |
| g. underground | ___ intersection |
| h. city centre | ___ freeway |
| i. torch | ___ sidewalk |
| j. timetable | ___ drugstore |
| k. solicitor | ___ railroad |
| l. chemist's | ___ faucet |
| m. tick | ___ zipper |
| n. tap | ___ attorney |
| o. zip | ___ downtown |

## 48. Hello Goodbye Welche Sätze passen zusammen?

a. *Good morning Mr. Murphy.*
b. *Hello Frank.*
c. *How are you?*
d. *I'm very glad to see you.*
e. *May I introduce you to Ms. Black?*
f. *Where are you from?*
g. *What do you do for a living?*
h. *It's getting rather late.*
i. *Thank you for a lovely evening!*
j. *Don't forget to keep in touch.*
k. *Give my regards to your wife.*
l. *Have a save journey home!*
m. *Thanks again, Cheerio!*
n. *Good bye, then.*
o. *I haven't seen you in a while!*

1. *I'm a consultant.*
2. *Cheerio!*
3. *Yes, it's been a long time!*
4. *You are welcome. I enjoyed it, too.*
5. *I won't. I'll give you a call next week.*
6. *I will. I'll say hello from you.*
7. *Good morning Mr. Gallagher.*
8. *Yes, I'll drive carefully.*
9. *Hi Helen. How are things?*
10. *Bye, bye.*
11. *It's a pleasure to meet you.*
12. *I'm fine, and yourself?*
13. *Me too. It's been a long time!*
14. *I'm from South Africa.*
15. *Yes, it is. I'd better go now.*

Lösung 49: a. know b. weather c. talk d. moment e. way f. word g. have h. friend i. introduce j. met k. around l. yet m. Pardon n. spare o. hand

Lösung 48: a. 7 b. 9 c. 12 d. 13 e. 11 f. 14 g. 1 h. 15 i. 4 j. 5 k. 6 l. 8 m. 2 n. 10 o. 3

## 49. Starting a Conversation Welche Wörter passen in die Lücken?

a. *Excuse me, but don't I ______ you?*
b. *Lovely ______ we're having, isn't it?*
c. *I'd like to ______ to you for a minute, if you've got time.*
d. *Have you got a ______? I'd like to ask you something.*
e. *By the ______, my name is Joanna.*
f. *Could I have a ______ with you.*
g. *I'd like to ______ a chat with you.*
h. *Excuse me, but aren't you a ______ of John's?*
i. *May I ______ myself. My name is Barry.*
j. *Haven't we ______ before?*
k. *I haven't seen you ______ here before.*
l. *Hi, we haven't been introduced ______. I'm Claire.*
m. *______ me, could I ask you a question?*
n. *Sorry, could you ______ a few minutes?*
o. *Could you give me a ______ with this, please?*

**spare**
**introduce**
**have**
**moment**
**weather**
**know**
**talk**
**way**
**word**
**friend**
**hand**
**met**
**yet**
**around**
**pardon**

## 50. WHAT A COINCIDENCE! Bringen Sie die Unterhaltung in die richtige Reihenfolge!

a. *I know her from work. What's your name?*
b. *Yes, I am. That's true! How do you know her?*
c. *Excuse me. Don't I know you from somewhere?*
d. *I've been to college with her. And you?*
e. *That's strange. I was sure you were one of Helen's friends.*
f. *I don't think so.*
g. *Yes, I know how that feels! Would you like to go for a pint?*
h. *O.K. Let's go then.*
i. *Well, I like it very much. But I still feel homesick at times.*
j. *Almost three months.*
k. *And how are you finding it here?*
l. *Mine is Andrea. How long have you been here now?*
m. *Oh, yes. That would be lovely.*
n. *My name is Oliver, and yours?*

Lösung 51: a. again b. mind c. slowly d. mean e. that f. beg g. understood h. What i. explain j. trying k. word l. whatever m. other n. correctly o. see

Lösung 50: c - f - e - b - d - a - n - l - j - k - i - g - m - h

## 51. Maintaining a Conversation Was passt in die Lücken?

| | |
|---|---|
| a. Could you say that ______ please? | **word** |
| b. Would you ______ repeating that? | **trying** |
| c. Could you speak more ______, please? | **what** |
| d. What do you ______ by ...? | **see** |
| e. What was ______? | **understood** |
| f. I ______ your pardon? | **beg** |
| g. I'm not sure I've ______ you correctly. | **slowly** |
| h. ______ do you think? | **mind** |
| i. Could you ______ what you mean? | **again** |
| j. How shall I put it? What I'm ______ to say is ... | **mean** |
| k. It's - what's the ______ - ... er ... | **that** |
| l. It's a ... or ______ it's called. | **explain** |
| m. In ______ words, it's ... | **whatever** |
| n. If I've understood you ______, you mean that ... | **correctly** |
| o. Oh yes, I ______ what you mean. | **other** |

## 52. Being polite Welche Sätze passen am besten zusammen?

*a. Would you like another piece of cake?*
*b. Could you pass me the salt, please.*
*c. This tastes absolutely delicious.*
*d. Does this dress suit me?*
*e. You've got a lovely house.*
*f. Thank you for all your help.*
*g. Would you like to go for dinner some night?*
*h. Do you mind if I borrow your car tonight?*
*i. Happy birthday Mr. Jones!*
*j. Good luck in your exams!*
*k. I'm awfully sorry, but I've lost your paper.*
*l. Please accept my apologies!*
*m. Merry Christmas and a happy new year!*
*o. Excuse me, you are standing on my foot.*

*1. Thanks. I'll need it.*
*2. I'm so sorry. Did I hurt you?*
*3. Thank's very much. Same to you.*
*4. Don't mention it!*
*5. You look marvelous in it!*
*6. Don't worry. I've got another copy.*
*7. No need to apologize!*
*8. Yes, of course. Here you are.*
*9. Yes, please. I'd love another one.*
*10. I'd be delighted to.*
*11. Do you think so? Thanks a lot.*
*12. How nice of you to remember it.*
*13. I'm glad you like it.*
*14. I'm really sorry, but I need it myself.*

Lösung 53: a. afraid b. talking c. together d. discuss e. now f. already g. interrupt h. lovely i. meet j. ring k. Thanks l. regards m. soon n. Safe o. best

Lösung 52: a. 9 b. 8 c. 13 d. 5 e. 11 f. 4 g. 10 h. 15 i. 12 j. 1 k. 6 l. 7 m. 3 n. 2

## 53. Ending a Conversation Welche Wörter gehören in die Lücken?

a. *I'm ______ I have to go now.*
b. *It's been great fun ______ to you.*
c. *We have to get ______ again.*
d. *We must ______ this again.*
e. *I really have to go ______.*
f. *Oh, goodness! It's ______ so late?*
g. *I hate to ______ you but I really have to go now.*
h. *Well, it's been ______ talking to you.*
i. *When could we ______ again?*
j. *Give me a ______ some time.*
k. *______ for coming.*
l. *Give my ______ to your whole family.*
m. *Hope to see you ______!*
n. *______ journey home!*
o. *All the ______!*

**best**
**safe**
**ring**
**meet**
**interrupt**
**discuss**
**talking**
**already**
**afraid**
**together**
**now**
**lovely**
**thanks**
**regards**
**soon**

## 54. MAKING EXCUSES Welche Sätze passen am besten zusammen?

*a. Why are you so late?*
*b. Did you miss your train again?*
*c. Why didn't you take a taxi?*
*d. Did the meeting finish late?*
*e. What's wrong with you?*
*f. Did you ring your mother last night?*
*g. Why didn't you ring me?*
*h. Did you write that letter?*
*i. I'm awfully sorry.*
*j. I'm sorry, but I won't make it tonight.*

*1. Oh, that's a pity! Maybe another time then.*
*2. Sorry, I didn't have time. I'll write it tomorrow.*
*3. Don't worry. It's alright.*
*4. I completely forgot! I better ring her now.*
*5. I was held up in traffic.*
*6. I tried, but your line was engaged all the time.*
*7. No I didn't. But it was delayed for half an hour.*
*8. There weren't any at the taxi rank.*
*9. Yes, we were still negotiating after 9 pm.*
*10. I don't feel well. I've got a terrible headache.*

Lösung 55: a. anything b. something c. anything d. anywhere e. some f. something h. Someone i. something j. some k. Anything l. any m. some n. some o. anyway

Lösung 54: a. 5 b. 7 c. 8 d. 9 e. 10 f. 4 g. 6 h. 2 i. 3 j. 1

## 55. Some or any? Was gehört in die Lücken?

a. *Did you do ______ interesting today?*
b. *I went shopping. I'm looking for ______ for Lisa's birthday.*
c. *I've been looking everywhere but I couldn't find ______.*
d. *Is there a bookshop ______ around here?*
e. *There are ______ good ones in this area.*
f. *But shouldn't we get ______ to eat first?*
g. *Good idea, I haven't eaten ______ all day.*
h. *______ told me this cafe over there is nice.*
i. *Would you like to order ______?*
j. *Yes, I'd like ______ tea please.*
k. *______ else?*
l. *Yes, do you have ______ cake?*
m. *It was good to get ______ rest, wasn't it?*
n. *Yes, it was ______ busy day today!*
o. *It was raining. But it was a nice trip, ______.*

## 56. Making a Phone Call

Bringen Sie die Wörter in die richtige Reihenfolge!

a. box is nearest where the phone

b. I call a make telephone where can

c. your I may telephone use

d. for I number dial what do Germany

e. cost what call local does a

f. she's not afraid moment the at I'm here

g. time rate start what cheap does the

Lösung 57: d - g - f - a - e - c - b und k - j - h - m - l - i

Lösung 56: a. Where is the nearest phone box? b. Where can I make a telephone call? c. May I use your telephone? d. What number do I dial for Germany? e. What does a local call cost? f. I'm afraid she's not here at the moment. g. What time does the cheap rate start?

## 57. Appointments

Bringen Sie die beiden Dialoge in die richtige Reihenfolge!

a. *I'm sorry, he'll be in meetings all day that day. How about the following Monday?*
b. *Yes, that suits me fine. Thank you very much. Good bye.*
c. *What about three o'clock?*
d. *Hello, I would like to make an appointment with Mr. Green, please.*
e. *Yes, I'm free that day. At what time?*
f. *Next Friday, if that's possible?*
g. *Yes, when would you like to see him?*
h. *Yes, let's do that. Would next Tuesday at eleven o'clock suit you?*
i. *O.K., see you then! Bye, bye.*
j. *I think this is probably best discussed face to face. Shall we arrange a meeting?*
k. *We have a problem with the new system. Can I ask you a few questions?*
l. *Eleven thirty is fine with me, too.*
m. *Let me check my diary. Actually, half past eleven would suit me better!*

## 58. With or without? Welches "that" kann weggelassen werden?

a. *I work for a company **that** makes computer software.*
b. *I like this dress **that** I only bought recently.*
c. *This is the worst film **that** I've ever seen.*
d. *Where is the cheese **that** was in the fridge?*
e. *Everything **that** she said was true.*
f. *Have you finished the work **that** you had to do?*
g. *The offices **that** are on the second floor are very small.*
h. *Do you know the woman **that** Tony is talking to?*
i. *Have you found the keys **that** you lost?*
j. *Why do you blame me for everything **that** goes wrong?*
k. ***That** is the woman I told you about.*
l. *The woman **that** lives next door is very friendly.*
m. *Is there anything else **that** I can do for you?*
n. *I like the people **that** I am working with.*
o. *I'm very disappointed **that** he forgot my birthday.*

Lösung 59: a. I don't agree with you at all. b. I'm sorry, but I have to refuse. c. We do not see eye to eye. d. That is totally out of the question.e. I am sure that you are mistaken. f. I am sorry, but you are wrong. g. I'm afraid I don't agree with you.

Lösung 58: a. that b. (that) c. (that) d. that e. (that) f. (that) g. that h. (that) i. (that) j. that k. That l. that m. (that) n. (that) o. that
Alle „that" in Klammern können weggelassen werden.

## 59. I beg to Differ! Wie lauten die Sätze?

a. at | I | you | all | agree | with | don't

b. but | to | I'm | have | refuse | sorry | I

c. eye | do | we | see | eye | to | not

d. question | of | out | is | the | that | totally

e. you | sure | are | I | mistaken | that | am

f. wrong | you | I | sorry | are | am | but

g. you | agree | with | afraid | don't | I'm | I

## 60. WHO'S CALLING? Welche Sätze passen am besten zusammen?

| | |
|---|---|
| a. *Who's calling?* | 1. *It's B-Y-R-N-E.* |
| b. *Can I take a message?* | 2. *No. I think you've got the wrong number.* |
| c. *How do you spell that?* | 3. *No, thanks. I'll call again later.* |
| d. *Can I speak to Andy, please?* | 4. *Yes, I'll put you through to her voicemail.* |
| e. *When will he be back?* | 5. *Yes, speaking. How can I help you?* |
| f. *Hello, am I speaking to the manager?* | 6. *Not until tomorrow morning, I'm afraid.* |
| g. *Who did you talk to earlier?* | 7. *Yes, half past three suits me fine.* |
| h. *Can I take down your number?* | 8. *I think it was Mr. Thompson.* |
| i. *Can I call you back?* | 9. *Yes, certainly. It's 365.* |
| j. *The line is busy. Please don't hang up.* | 10. *Yes. I'll be here until 7 o'clock tonight.* |
| k. *Is this the flight information?* | 11. *Thank you, too. Good bye.* |
| l. *Could you call again at 3.30?* | 12. *No problem. I'll hold.* |
| m. *Thank you for calling.* | 13. *My name is Nicola Morris.* |
| n. *May I have your extension, please?* | 14. *I'm afraid he's not in at the moment.* |
| o. *Could I have a message for her?* | 15. *Yes, it's New York 753 8968.* |

Lösung 61: a. would happen b. used c. would arrive d. would have come e. had had f. didn't g. would buy h. spoke i. will get j. was k. would move l. had seen m. hadn't helped n. drove o. tell

Lösung 60: a. 13 b. 3 c. 1 d. 14 e. 6 f. 5 g. 8 h. 15 i. 10 j. 12 k. 2 l. 7 m. 11 n. 9 o. 4

## 61. If–Clauses Setzen Sie die richtige Verbform ein!

a. *What (happen) ______ if I pressed that red button?*
b. *Would you mind if I (use) ______ your phone?*
c. *If we took the ten o'clock train, we (arrive) ______ too early.*
d. *If I had known you were in hospital I (come) ______ to visit you.*
e. *If you (have) ______ your breakfast, you wouldn't be hungry now.*
f. *We'd visit you more often if you (do) ______ live so far away.*
g. *If I were you I (buy) ______ that coat.*
h. *People would understand you better if you (speak) ______ more clearly.*
i. *If you can speak a foreign language, you (get) ______ a job more easily.*
j. *I wouldn't mind living in England if the weather (be) ______ a bit better.*
k. *If we had the choice, we (move) ______ to the country side.*
l. *If I (see) ______ you I would have said 'hello'.*
m. *I don't know what I would have done if you (not help) ______ me.*
n. *If people (drive) ______ with more care there would be less accidents.*
o. *I will meet you at the pub if you (tell) ______ me how to get there.*

## 62. LOOK AND SEE Setzen Sie die Ausdrücke in ihrer korrekten Form ein!

| | | |
|---|---|---|
| a. | *You and your sister <u>have a similar appearance</u>.* → ______ | **look after** |
| b. | *Travelling in the rush hour, <u>beware of</u> pickpockets!* → ______ | **see eye to eye** |
| c. | *He <u>regards</u> many people <u>as inferior</u>.* → ______ | **look for** |
| d. | *A group of <u>curious people</u> had gathered after the accident.* → ______ | **sightseers** |
| e. | *If you don't know a word, <u>refer to</u> a dictionary!* → ______ | **give someone a funny look** |
| f. | *Promise me that you will <u>take care of</u> yourself!* → ______ | **look something up in** |
| g. | *When she called him an idiot he <u>went totally mad</u>.* → ______ | **look back on** |
| h. | *This story was a pack of lies and we all <u>disbelieved it</u>.* → ______ | **onlookers** |
| i. | *A day ticket is the best way for <u>tourists</u> to get around here.* → ______ | **look down on** |
| j. | *We got a lovely room <u>with a view of</u> the sea.* → ______ | **overlook** |
| k. | *Old people like to <u>remember</u> their younger days.* → ______ | **see through it** |
| l. | *Best friends don't always <u>agree</u> on everything.* → ______ | **look alike** |
| m. | *She <u>glanced at me strangely</u>.* → ______ | **look out for** |
| n. | *Can you help me <u>searching my</u> keys?* → ______ | **see red** |
| o. | *I <u>won't take account</u> of your misbehaviour.* → ______ | **overlooking** |

Lösung 63: a. larger b. nicest c. the highest d. higher e. the poorest f. worse g. most popular h. more popular i. more comfortable j. the quickest k. faster l. happier m. the eldest n. older o. the best

Lösung 62: a. look alike b. look out for c. looks down on d. onlookers e. look it up in f. look after g. saw red h. saw through i. sightseers j. overlooking k. look back on l. see eye to eye m. gave me a funny look n. looking for o. will overlook

## 63. Comparisons Setzen Sie die korrekte Form ein!

a. *The United States are very large. But Canada is ___________ (large).*
b. *She is lovely, one of the ___________ (nice) people I know.*
c. *Mount Everest is ___________ (high) mountain in the world.*
d. *It is ___________ (high) than any other mountain.*
e. *Mali is one of ___________ (poor) countries in the world.*
f. *But people in Ethiopia are even (bad) ___________ off.*
g. *What is the ___________ (popular) sport in your country?*
h. *Football is much ___________ (popular) than basketball here.*
i. *I prefer this chair. It's much ___________ (comfortable).*
j. *What's ___________ (quick) way to the station?*
k. *You can walk down here but you're ___________ (fast) if you take the bus.*
l. *He was a bit depressed but he looks ___________ (happy) now.*
m. *Are you ___________ (old) in your family?*
n. *No, I've got two ___________ (old) brothers.*
o. *That's ___________(good) film I've ever seen.*

## 64. What's the Time? Was passt in die Lücken?

| | |
|---|---|
| a. *Excuse me. Can you please ______ me what time it is?* | **week** |
| b. *It's exactly four ______.* | **hour** |
| c. *Sorry, ______ time do you close?* | **start** |
| d. *At six in the evening on ______ and at noon on Saturdays.* | **already** |
| e. *Is this the right ______?* | **time** |
| f. *No, this clock is ten minutes ______.* | **o'clock** |
| g. *It's twenty to three ______? Oh, no! I'm going to be late.* | **what** |
| h. *What time does the concert ______?* | **tell** |
| i. *It starts in half an ______, at eight p.m. sharp.* | **weekdays** |
| j. *Excuse me! What's the ______ today?* | **of** |
| k. *It's the 23rd ______ June.* | **slow** |
| l. *What day do they ______ back the clock?* | **date** |
| m. *It's ______ time in April, isn't it?* | **definitely** |
| n. *What's your favourite day of the ______?* | **some** |
| o. *That would ______ be Sunday!* | **turn** |

Lösung 65: a. for b. for c. since d. since e. since f. for g. since h. for i. for j. for k. for l. since m. for n. for o. since

Lösung 64: a. tell b. o'clock c. what d. weekdays e. time f. slow g. already h. start i. hour j. date k. of l. turn m. some n. week m. definitely

## 65. HOBBIES Setzen Sie "since" oder "for" ein!

a. *I have been playing the guitar ______ over ten years.*
b. *I go jogging ______ half an hour every morning.*
c. *I'm a member of this football club ______ the fifties.*
d. *I have loved swimming ______ I was a child.*
e. *I have not been wind-surfing ______ our last holiday in France.*
f. *I have been trying to learn how to cook ______ ages.*
g. *I have been studying English ______ 1992.*
h. *Let's go walking ______ an hour!*
i. *I haven't been practising the piano ______ a long time.*
j. *I could stay in a museum ______ hours.*
k. *They have been renovating their house ______ more than 4 months.*
l. *I started to love gardening ______ we moved into our new house.*
m. *Have you arranged that fishing trip ______ next Sunday?*
n. *Have you been playing golf ______ a long time?*
o. *No, I'm only doing it ______ last spring.*

## 66. Ready, Steady, Cook! Setzen sie die richtigen Wörter ein!

a. *Where else would you cook but in the ______.*
b. *Good quality fresh ______ are essential for a successful meal.*
c. *You should sharpen your ______ before preparing ingredients.*
d. *If you aren't a great cook, a good ______ might be useful.*
e. *Protect your worktop with a ______ board.*
f. *You can't do without ______.*
g. *Some ______ demand that you preheat your oven.*
h. *To avoid making fatty meals, you should ______ your meat.*
i. *Complete this idiom: Too many ______ spoil the broth.*
j. *Some people like their potatoes sauteed but I like mine ______.*
k. *The traditional English way to eat sausage is ______.*
l. *Bon appetit! or Enjoy your ______!*
m. *Most people hate to wash ______ after dinner.*
n. *Children usually don't like too ______ food.*

***ingredients***
***fried***
***cookbook***
***recipes***
***kitchen***
***dishes***
***chopping***
***grill***
***knives***
***spicy***
***boiled***
***cooks***
***salt & pepper***
***meal***

Lösung 67: a. had two teeth knocked out. b. had/got them fixed c. have our carpets cleaned. d. have them delivered e. had his car repaired f. have the report copied g. have it put h. have your children vaccinated i. had my ears tested j. has her hair done k. having new bushes planted l. have the old ones pulled out. m. have your homework done n. have the air-condition checked. o. have the computer repaired.

Lösung 66: a. kitchen b. ingredients c. knives d. cookbook e. chopping f. salt & pepper g. recipes h. grill i. cooks j. boiled k. fried l. meal m. dishes n. spicy

## 67. Having something done Lassen Sie's andere tun!

a. *He (two teeth/knock out) ___________.*
b. *But he (them/fix) ___________ at the dentist the next day.*
c. *We'd like to (our carpets/clean) ___________.*
d. *Could we (them/deliver) ___________ by tomorrow?*
e. *He (his car/repair) ___________ several times this year.*
f. *Could I (the report/copy) ___________, please?*
g. *I'll (it/put) ___________ on your desk by noon.*
h. *You should (children/vaccinate) ___________ against the flu.*
i. *I (ears/test) ___________ last month.*
j. *She (her hair/do) ___________ every Saturday.*
k. *We are (new bushes/plant) ___________ in the garden.*
l. *But first we must (old ones/ pull out) ___________.*
m. *You mustn't (your homework/do) ___________ by somebody else!*
n. *We should (air-condition/check) ___________.*
o. *It was too expensive to (computer/repair) ___________.*

## 68. LET'S DO IT! Setzen Sie "DO" und "MAKE" in der richtigen Form ein!

a. *Let's think how we can ______ the best of the situation!*
b. *Can you ______ the shopping today?*
c. *I expect you to ______ your best.*
d. *I think I'll ______ her a cake for her birthday.*
e. *Why am I always ______ the same stupid mistakes?*
f. *I've started ______ some painting with oil colours recently.*
g. *We better ______ plans for our holidays soon.*
h. *He ______ a habit of going for a pint after work.*
i. *Have they ______ arrangements for their wedding yet?*
j. *Could you ______ me a favour, please?*
k. *I can't come tonight because I have to ______ an exam tomorrow.*
l. *It will ______ you no harm to do a little bit of work.*
m. *Have you ______ big improvements studying English?*
n. *We better ______ a decision quickly.*
o. *At least we have ______ an effort to help.*

Lösung 69: a. falsch (boss/supervisor) b. richtig c. falsch (sensitive) d. falsch (nearest) e. richtig f. richtig g. falsch (latest) h. falsch (high school/secondary school) i. falsch (murderer) j. richtig k. falsch (jam) l. falsch (invested) m. richtig n. falsch (inhumane) o. richtig

Lösung 68: a. make b. do c. do d. make e. making f. doing g. make h. makes i. made j. do k. do l. do m. made n. make o. made

## 69. True or false? Welche Sätze sind richtig, welche falsch?

a. *I will have to get this holiday request approved by my chef first.* richtig – falsch
b. *I wonder how you can be so energetic all the time.* richtig – falsch
c. *She's so sensible, when you say something wrong she starts crying.* richtig – falsch
d. *Can you please tell me the way to the next post office?* richtig – falsch
e. *The first regiment is stationed in York.* richtig – falsch
f. *His heart was heavy with sorrow.* richtig – falsch
g. *They always show the actual news first on this channel.* richtig – falsch
h. *I spent 9 years at gymnasium before I went to university.* richtig – falsch
i. *He's a murder, he killed six people.* richtig – falsch
j. *His paintings are in the Neo-Modern style.* richtig – falsch
k. *I love strawberry marmelade for breakfast.* richtig – falsch
l. *Our company investigated a lot of money into this project.* richtig – falsch
m. *The repairs where carried out by him.* richtig – falsch
n. *The treatment of prisoners in this country is inhuman.* richtig – falsch
o. *He's very sociable, he makes new friends very quickly.* richtig – falsch

## 70. The Weather Setzen Sie die richtigen Wörter ein!

a. *It's a lovely day _ _ _ _ _, isn't it?*
b. *Yes. _ _ _ _ _ better than yesterday.*
c. *It's indeed fairly mild for this _ _ _ _ _ of the year.*
d. *Yes, quite different from the _ _ _ _ _.*
e. *They _ _ _ _ _ heavy showers and strong winds for today.*
f. *But it doesn't _ _ _ _ _ like it's going to rain.*
g. *I hope it stays fine for the _ _ _ _ _!*
h. *It's supposed to turn _ _ _ _ _ the next days.*
i. *They say the _ _ _ _ _ will drop to around zero.*
j. *And it _ _ _ _ _ even snow on Sunday.*
k. *Yes, I thought it wouldn't _ _ _ _ _.*
l. *How many _ _ _ _ _ is it, do you know?*
m. *It must be _ _ _ _ _ 5 degrees (centigrades).*
n. *It's a very severe _ _ _ _ _ this year.*
o. *I hope it's going to be _ _ _ _ _ by an early spring.*

**around**
**degrees**
**temperatures**
**colder**
**look**
**forecast**
**time**
**followed**
**much**
**today**
**predicted**
**weekend**
**might**
**last**
**winter**

Lösung 71: a. 2 b. 1 c. 3 d. 2 e. 3 f. 1

Lösung 70: a. today b. Much c. time d. forecast e. predicted f. look g. weekend h. colder i. temperatures j. might k. last l. degrees m. around n. winter o. followed

## 71. Talking about the Family Welche Antwort ist die richtige?

*a. Have you got any children?*

1. *Yes, I'm having two boys.*
2. *Yes, I have two boys.*
3. *Yes, I have any.*

*b. How old is your youngest?*

1. *He's going to be 17 next month.*
2. *He is been 17 next month.*
3. *He has 17 years.*

*c. And your eldest, what does he do?*

1. *He has working for the government.*
2. *He is working for the government.*
3. *He works for the government.*

*d. Is he married?*

1. *Yes, his wife is going to expect twins.*
2. *Yes, his wife is expecting twins.*
3. *Yes, his wife is expected twins.*

*e. Do your parents still live together?*

1. *No, they have devorcing now.*
2. *Now, they are devorcing now.*
3. *No, they are devorced now.*

*f. And your parents-in-law?*

1. *The get on really well.*
2. *They are getting on really well.*
3. *They are got on really well.*

## 72. All the Relatives Wie lauten die Sätze?

a. any sisters you have and got brothers

b. older two got have brothers I

c. do and living they what do a for

d. both are college they in still

e. any have do city relatives this in you

f. is school daughter still primary my in

g. only I an am child

Lösung 73: a. themselves b. himself c. myself d. yourself e. myself f. herself g. yourself h. ourselves i. itself j. yourself k. himself l. herself m. myself n. yourselves o. –

Lösung 72: a. Have you got any sisters and brothers? b. I have got two older brothers. c. And what do they do for a living? d. They both are still in college. e. Do you have any relatives in this city? f. My daughter is still in primary school. g. I am an only child.

## 73. Do it yourself! Wie muss es heißen?

a. *Are Jean and Andy going to renovate the house all by ______?*
b. *He can't repair the car ______.*
c. *I never clean the windows ______.*
d. *It's up to ______, Frank!*
e. *I haven't got time to type this up ______.*
f. *The girl at the reception doesn't fix the air-condition ______.*
g. *You look tired, mom. You should take better care of ______.*
h. *Mike and me baked this cake ______.*
i. *Do you think the table is going to lay ______?*
j. *Mary, what have you done to______?*
k. *I don't know his name. He never introduced ______!*
l. *Don't you think that she is letting ______ go?*
m. *I couldn't imagine ______ standing on this stage.*
n. *Enjoy ______, children! I wish you a great time!*
o. *Let's meet ______ at five then.*

## 74. Talking about Work

Formulieren Sie die Sätze!

a. living for do you what do a

b. moment I'm an doing apprenticeship at the

c. have a to I lot people do with

d. for company work you what do

e. regional for I authorities work the

f. challenge is job real my a sometimes

g. you job can detail in describe more your

Lösung 75: a. like b. awful c. happened d. wrong e. Tell f. late g. sick h. broke i. meeting j. pay rise k. argument l. about m. remember n. relax o. darling

Lösung 74: a. What do you do for a living? b. At the moment I'm doing an apprenticeship. c. I have a lot to do with people. d. What company do you work for? e. I work for the regional authorities. f. Sometimes my job is a real challenge. g. Can you describe your job in more detail?

## 75. A BAD DAY! Füllen Sie die Lücken!

a. *What was your day at work _ _ _?*
b. *Oh, it was _ _ _!*
c. *Why, what _ _ _?*
d. *It was really stressfull, and just about everything went _ _ _ today.*
e. *Oh, really? _ _ _ me about it!*
f. *Well, first of all the traffic was so bad that I was half an hour _ _ _ this morning.*
g. *When I arrived I learned that my secretary was _ _ _ and wouldn't be in.*
h. *Just after I had finished typing the report my computer _ _ _ down.*
i. *After lunch I had a _ _ _ with my boss and couldn't find the right room.*
j. *Then my boss told me I wouldn't get the _ _ _ I had expected.*
k. *I also had a stupid _ _ _ with one of my colleagues.*
l. *What was it _ _ _?*
m. *I can't even _ _ _. It was just such a bad day altogether!*
n. *Why don't you sit down and _ _ _, and I'll make you a nice cup of tea?*
o. *You're a _ _ _!*

***remember***
***about***
***pay rise***
***sick***
***wrong***
***like***
***awful***
***happened***
***darling***
***broke***
***meeting***
***relax***
***argument***
***tell***
***late***

## 76. Talking about Music Was passt in die Lücken?

| | |
|---|---|
| a. *What kind of music do you _ _ _ _ _ to?* | **record** |
| b. *It's difficult to say. I like all _ _ _ _ _ of music.* | **practiced** |
| c. *I listen to _ _ _ _ _ really: pop music, oldies, easy listening...* | **instrument** |
| d. *What type of music do you like _ _ _ _ _?* | **bought** |
| e. *My _ _ _ _ _ type of music is folk.* | **play** |
| f. *I love this song, it's a _ _ _ _ _ piece.* | **favorite** |
| g. *I really hate this song they constantly _ _ _ _ _ on the radio.* | **best** |
| h. *I _ _ _ _ _ this jazz album the other day. It's absolutely brilliant.* | **anything** |
| i. *I love _ _ _ _ _ music, especially operas.* | **choir** |
| j. *I can't _ _ _ _ _ Country and Western. I really hate it.* | **classical** |
| k. *Do you play an _ _ _ _ _?* | **listen** |
| l. *I used to play the piano, but I gave it up cause I never _ _ _ _ _.* | **kinds** |
| m. *My brother plays in a _ _ _ _ _, he's the singer and bass player.* | **classic** |
| n. *He's got quite an impressive _ _ _ _ _ collection.* | **stand** |
| o. *I used to sing in the school _ _ _ _ _.* | **band** |

Lösung 77: a. interested b. kinds c. enjoy d. martial e. armchair f. match g. stadium h. home i. sounds j. half past two k. badly l. second half m. score n. chances o. beat

Lösung 76: a. listen b. kinds c. anything d. best e. favorite f. classic g. play h. bought i. classical j. stand k. instrument l. practiced m. band n. record o. choir

## 77. Very Sporty Füllen Sie die Lücken!

| | |
|---|---|
| a. *Are you _ _ _ _ _ in sports?* | **second half** |
| b. *Yes, I'm interested in most _ _ _ _ _ of sport.* | **sounds** |
| c. *I play tennis myself and I _ _ _ _ _ hiking and mountain climbing.* | **beat** |
| d. *I also like the _ _ _ _ _ arts, I used to do Karate. What about you?* | **home** |
| e. *I'm more an _ _ _ _ _ sportsman, but I do play golf and snooker.* | **match** |
| f. *Would you like to go to the soccer _ _ _ _ _ with me next Sunday?* | **martial** |
| g. *Yes, I'd like to. I haven't been to the new _ _ _ _ _ yet. Who's playing?* | **kinds** |
| h. *The two teams at the top of the table. It's a _ _ _ _ _ game.* | **interested** |
| i. *That _ _ _ _ _ marvellous! What time does it start at?* | **enjoy** |
| j. *At three o'clock, but we should be there at _ _ _ _ _.* | **armchair** |
| k. *Our team is playing _ _ _ _ _ today!* | **stadium** |
| l. *They are playing better in the _ _ _ _ _ than in the first.* | **half past two** |
| m. *The _ _ _ _ _ is five to two. There's no doubt who's going to win.* | **score** |
| n. *They missed several good _ _ _ _ _. I must say I'm a bit disappointed.* | **chances** |
| o. *Next time we're going to _ _ _ _ _ them!* | **badly** |

## 78. THE NEW HOUSE Welche Wörter passen in die Lücken?

| | |
|---|---|
| a. *You're all _ _ _ _, Laura. What's the matter?* | **grow** |
| b. *We've just _ _ _ _ a new house.* | **many** |
| c. *Oh, congratulations! Have you _ _ _ _ what you were looking for?* | **detached** |
| d. *Yes, it's _ _ _ _ what we had in mind.* | **about** |
| e. *It's bigger than our present house, and it's in a nice, quiet _ _ _ _.* | **found** |
| f. *And it's very _ _ _ _ for Derek's office. It'll only take him 20 minutes.* | **bought** |
| g. *Where _ _ _ _ is it?* | **excited** |
| h. *In Blanchardstown, off the Navan road. It's in a newly _ _ _ _ estate.* | **exactly** |
| i. *That's a nice _ _ _ _. Very close to the country side. What's the house like?* | **convenient** |
| j. *It's lovely. It's semi _ _ _ _ and very spacious.* | **reasonable** |
| k. *How _ _ _ _ rooms has it got?* | **area** |
| l. *Three bedrooms, a living room, a _ _ _ _ room, a study and a kitchen.* | **always** |
| m. *What about the garden? You _ _ _ _ wanted a large garden, didn't you?* | **neighbourhood** |
| n. *Oh, it's huge. We might even be able to _ _ _ _ our own potatoes!* | **dining** |
| o. *We bought the house at a _ _ _ _ price.* | **developed** |

Lösung 79: a. If we had more money we would buy a bigger house in a suburb. b. If we bought a bigger house we wouldn't live in this neighbourhood. c. It would take me an hour to go to work if we lived in a suburb. d. If we lived in a bigger house we would have a lot more housework. e. We wouldn't really be happier if we had a bigger house.

Lösung 78: a. excited b. bought c. found d. exactly e. neighbourhood f. convenient g. about h. developed i. area j. detached k. many l. dining m. always n. grow

## 79. If Things were Different Wie lauten die Sätze?

a. *in a suburb / a bigger house / we / if we / would / had more money / buy*
*If* ______________________________________________

b. *bought a bigger house / we / live / in this neighbourhood / if / we wouldn't*
*If* ______________________________________________

c. *take me an hour / we / it / in a suburb / if / lived / to get to work / would*
*It* ______________________________________________

d. *a lot more housework / lived / we / have / if / in a bigger house / would / we*
*If* ______________________________________________

e. *happier / had / we / we / wouldn't really / a bigger house / be / if*
*We* ______________________________________________

## 80. Home sweet Home Füllen Sie die Lücken?

a. *Where do you _ _ _ _?*
b. *I live in a _ _ _ _ in the country.*
c. *That _ _ _ _ be very nice!*
d. *Oh yes, it's a very quiet _ _ _ _. I'm glad we moved out of the city.*
e. *How long have you been _ _ _ _ there now?*
f. *For almost ten years. We _ _ _ _ in soon after we got married.*
g. *Are you _ _ _ _?*
h. *No, it's our own house. But we're still paying off the _ _ _ _.*
i. *And _ _ _ _ do you live?*
j. *I'm _ _ _ _ a flat with friends from college. Before, I used to live in lodgings.*
k. *My old _ _ _ _ was very strict. She didn't allow female visitors!*
l. *You must be glad to have some more freedom now! What's your _ _ _ _ like?*
m. *It's on the _ _ _ _ floor. It has three bedrooms, a kitchen and a bathroom.*
n. *Is it in the _ _ _ _ of town?*
o. *No, it's in the _ _ _ _. But it's very convenient to public transport.*

**ground**
**flat**
**suburbs**
**sharing**
**where**
**renting**
**living**
**must**
**house**
**live**
**environment**
**moved**
**mortgage**
**landlady**
**centre**

Lösung 81: a. to having b. going c. to go d. repeating e. talking f. to get g. to go h. asking i. to answer j. to hearing k. to interrupt l. to getting m. to get n. using o. to lock

Lösung 80: a. live b. house c. must d. environment e. living f. moved g. renting h. mortgage i. where j. sharing k. landlady l. flat m. ground n. centre o. suburbs

## 81. How do you say it? Streichen Sie die richtige Lösung an!

a. *Are you looking forward* ***to have/having/to having*** *a holiday next month?*
b. *I've always dreamt about* ***to go/going/to going*** *to Australia.*
c. *I've never been to Australia but I'd love* ***to go/going/to going*** *there.*
d. *Would you mind* ***to repeat/repeating/to repeating*** *this sentence?*
e. *She's a very interesting person. I always enjoy* ***to talk/talking/to talking*** *to her.*
f. *They just announced that they decided* ***to get/getting/to getting*** *married.*
g. *It was a lovely day so we decided* ***to go/going/to going*** *for a walk.*
h. *Why do you keep* ***to ask/ asking/to asking*** *me questions?*
i. *I refuse* ***to answer/answering/to answering*** *any more of your questions!*
j. *I'm looking forward* ***to hear/hearing/to hearing*** *from you soon!*
k. *Forgive me* ***to interrupt/interrupting/to interrupting*** *you, but may I ask you something?*
l. *I just can't get used* ***to get/getting/to getting*** *up so early.*
m. *When I was younger I used* ***to get/getting/to getting*** *up early every day.*
n. *I don't mind you* ***to use/using/to using*** *the phone as long as you pay for it.*
o. *Please remember* ***to lock/locking/to locking*** *the door when you go out.*

## 82. Let's go for a Pint! Finden Sie die richtigen Wörter!

a. *Shall we go for a ______ this weekend?*
b. *What about going on a ______ with the lads?*
c. *Good idea. Which pub shall we ______ with?*
d. *What ______ The Red Lion?*
e. *No, the music is always too ______ there.*
f. *I like big, modern ______ where there's plenty of loud music.*
g. *I'd prefer ______ a little bit more quiet.*
h. *O.K. Let's try out that ______ place in high street.*
i. *What's it ______ in there?*
j. *I haven't been drinking there ______ yet.*
k. *But I ______ it's quite nice and cosy.*
l. *O.K. Let's ______ for it then.*
m. *I'll buy the first ______.*
n. *You're ______!*

**go**
**on**
**somewhere**
**start**
**drink**
**like**
**pub-crawl**
**about**
**pubs**
**loud**
**new**
**heard**
**myself**
**round**

Lösung 83: c - b - a - e - g - d - j - f - k - i - m - h - l

Lösung 82: a. drink b. pub-crawl c. start d. about e. loud f. pubs g. somewhere h. new i. like j. myself k. heard l. go m. round n. on

## 83. At the Pub Bringen Sie den Dialog in die richtige Reihenfolge!

a. *Don't you fancy a game of darts then?*
b. *Let's go to the lounge. There's always a game of dart going on in the bar.*
c. *Where shall we sit? At the bar or in the lounge?*
d. *I don't know. I don't feel too well. I think I've caught a cold.*
e. *No, I just want a quiet drink.*
f. *A pint of stout and a hot whiskey, please. And do you have some pub grub?*
g. *Let's sit down here then. I'll get the first round. What are you having?*
h. *Give me one each, please.*
i. *I'll have two packets of crisps then.*
j. *Then you should have a hot whiskey. That'll sort you out.*
k. *Only crisps and peanuts.*
l. *There you go. That's 5.45 altogether please.*
m. *Cheese and onion or salt and vinegar?*

## 84. "Mis-" or "Dis-"? Drücken Sie mit der passenden Vorsilbe das Gegenteil aus!

| | |
|---|---|
| a. I'm sure that it was not a mark of _ _ _ _ _ on his behalf. | satisfied |
| b. Excuse me sir, but due to a _ _ _ _ _ we seem to have over-charged your bill. | continued |
| c. It's not his fault that people always seem to _ _ _ _ _ him. | informed |
| d. While our car was being stolen, we could do nothing but watch in _ _ _ _ _. | fortune |
| e. The train had to be stopped after a _ _ _ _ _ between some passengers. | belief |
| f. I think that Chad needs a filofax to help him stop being so _ _ _ _ _. | trust |
| g. Mrs. Livingstone had never done a _ _ _ _ _ thing in her life. | respect |
| h. You won't get any Christmas presents if you continue to _ _ _ _ _ like this! | behave |
| i. I am afraid but this particular product has been _ _ _ _ _. | calculation |
| j. Unfortunately, that particular tourist seemed to have been woefully _ _ _ _ _. | understanding |
| k. The clerk informed us that we should _ _ _ _ _ all previous announcements. | organized |
| l. The _ _ _ _ _ of the emergency stop button carries a fine of £500. | honest |
| m. Do I have the right not to pay if I am _ _ _ _ _ with a restaurant's service? | regard |
| n. We had the _ _ _ _ _ to take our vacation during the monsoon season! | use |

Lösung 85: a. watch b. catching c. admit d. anything e. guide f. showing g. cinema h. documentary i. afterwards j. episode k. soaps l. season m. renting n. turn o. off

Lösung 84: a. disrespect b. miscalculation c. distrust d. disbelief e. misunderstanding f. disorganized g. dishonest h. misbehave i. discontinued j. misinformed k. disregard l. misuse m. dissatisfied n. misfortune

## 85. Anything on the telly tonight? Welche Wörter sind gesucht?

a. *Do you _ _ _ _ a lot of television?*
b. *Not much. It's practically for _ _ _ _ up on the news. That's all.*
c. *I must _ _ _ _ that I watch quite a lot.*
d. *Is there _ _ _ _ good on tonight?*
e. *Let's have a look into the TV _ _ _ _.*
f. *On Channel four they are _ _ _ _ a movie at ten thirty.*
g. *I've seen it before though. I saw it in the _ _ _ _ last summer.*
h. *I'd like to watch that _ _ _ _ about sharks on BBC 2.*
i. *And there is some comedy on _ _ _ _.*
j. *Did you see the last _ _ _ _ of Coronation Street?*
k. *I'm sorry, I don't watch _ _ _ _ at all.*
l. *There's not much on the telly during the silly _ _ _ _.*
m. *Yeah, we'd be better off _ _ _ _ a video.*
n. *Can you please _ _ _ _ the TV down a little bit?*
o. *Why don't we turn it _ _ _ _ altogether?*

***season***
***soaps***
***episode***
***documentary***
***turn***
***showing***
***guide***
***catching***
***watch***
***admit***
***anything***
***cinema***
***off***
***afterwards***
***renting***

## 86. PASSIVE Formulieren Sie die Sätze im Passiv!

a. *Somebody has cleaned the room.* ____________________

b. *They have postponed the concert.* ____________________

c. *Somebody is using the PC at the moment.* ____________________

d. *They had to cancel all flights.* ____________________

e. *They asked me some difficult questions.* ____________________

f. *They are building a new motorway.* ____________________

g. *Somebody cleans the rooms every day.* ____________________

h. *People don't use this road very often.* ____________________

i. *They advised us not to go out alone.* ____________________

j. *Someone accused me of stealing money.* ____________________

k. *Have you watered the flowers?* ____________________

l. *We must assume that he is telling the truth.* ____________________

m. *They didn't give me the money.* ____________________

n. *How much will they pay you?* ____________________

o. *Has anybody shown you what to do?* ____________________

Lösung 87: a. reading b. dailies c. novel d. author e. difficult f. translation g. detective h. exciting i. written j. read k. agree l. sensational m. like n. magazines o. subscription

Lösung 86: a. The rooms have been cleaned. b. The concert has been postponed. c. The PC is being used at the moment. d. All flights had to be cancelled. e. I was asked some difficult questions. f. A new motorway is being built. g. The rooms are cleaned every day. h. This road isn't used very often. i. We were advised not to go out alone. j. I was accused of stealing money. k. Have the flowers been watered? l. It must be assumed that he is telling the truth. m. I wasn't given the money. n. How much will you get paid? o. Have you been shown what to do?

## 87. A GOOD READ Füllen Sie die Lücken!

a. *What do you enjoy _ _ _ _?*
b. *It depends. During the week, I read the _ _ _ _.*
c. *But at the weekend or on holiday, I love to get lost in a good _ _ _ _.*
d. *Who's your favorite _ _ _ _?*
e. *That's _ _ _ _ to say. Perhaps Umberto Eco.*
f. *But I always find that his books lose a lot in _ _ _ _. I always try to read the original.*
g. *Oh, I find his books very heavy. I prefer love stories or _ _ _ _ novels like Ruth Rendell's.*
h. *I've never read a more _ _ _ _ book than her last one. I couldn't put it down.*
i. *You must read it! It's very well _ _ _ _. I can lend it to you if you want.*
j. *Have you _ _ _ _ the editorial in the paper today?*
k. *Yes, it's very controversial. Do you _ _ _ _ with the editor's opinion?*
l. *Not really. His _ _ _ _ style shouldn't be taken too seriously.*
m. *I have to say though that I _ _ _ _ his columns.*
n. *Which political _ _ _ _ are good?*
o. *I have a _ _ _ _ to Newsweek. That's ten percent cheaper than the newsstand price.*

## 88. MAKE & DO Setzen Sie den passenden Ausdruck in der richtigen Form ein!

| | | |
|---|---|---|
| a. I could hardly <u>understand</u> what she was saying. | ______ | make |
| b. Admit that you <u>invented</u> the whole story! | ______ | make out |
| c. The company I work for had <u>a celebration</u> last night. | ______ | do without |
| d. They <u>renovated</u> the whole house by themselves! | ______ | make way |
| e. One of the biggest hobbies is <u>home improvement</u>. | ______ | make do |
| f. This park will be destroyed to <u>provide space</u> for the road. | ______ | do up |
| g. I'll be glad when this affair is <u>completely finished</u>. | ______ | have nothing to do with |
| h. I find it easy to <u>manage without</u> a car in the city. | ______ | make-up |
| i. There are a few <u>rules</u> you should be aware of. | ______ | make up |
| j. We will have to <u>get by</u> with the money we have left. | ______ | a bit of a do |
| k. Thanks for the favour. I'll <u>return</u> it another time. | ______ | dos and don'ts |
| l. The government <u>abolished</u> nuclear weapons. | ______ | over and done with |
| m. What he told me <u>was irrelevant to</u> the subject. | ______ | make up for |
| n. They have a new car but I'm not sure what <u>brand</u> it is. | ______ | do away with |
| o. Can I pay for this at the <u>cosmetics</u> counter? | ______ | do-it-yourself |

Lösung 89: a. out of date b. technology c. equipment d. freak e. incredibly f. surfing g. contact h. favorite i. adding j. order k. download l. browser m. engines n. connecting

Lösung 88: a. make out b. made up c. a bit of a do d. did up e. do-it-yourself f. make way g. over and done with h. do without i. dos and don'ts j. make do k. make up for l. did away with m. had nothing to do with n. make o. make-up

## 89. The World of Computers Welche Wörter passen in die Lücken?

| | |
|---|---|
| a. *My son bought a computer last year and it's already ______.* | **engines** |
| b. *That's easy to believe. Computer ______ is growing so quickly.* | **connecting** |
| c. *My son always wants the best ______ and will spend all his money on it.* | **download** |
| d. *I'm a bit of a computer ______ myself. But my new machine is phantastic.* | **order** |
| e. *It has an ______ fast hard disk and great graphics.* | **favorite** |
| f. *I could spend hours in front of the screen ______ the net and chatting with friends.* | **contact** |
| g. *E-mail is so handy for staying in ______ but you also get a lot of junk-mails.* | **incredibly** |
| h. *I don't know. I still prefer snail mail. Do you have a ______ web side?* | **freak** |
| i. *I'm ______ to the list all the time. I found a very interesting one the other day.* | **technology** |
| j. *You can listen to new CDs and ______ them directly via the web.* | **out of date** |
| k. *There's also a possibility to ______ titles from the latest releases.* | **equipment** |
| l. *Which ______ do you think is the most effective for viewing web pages?* | **surfing** |
| m. *I find different search ______ are better for different subjects.* | **adding** |
| n. *The internet is very busy in the afternoon and ______ to a web side can take ages.* | **browser** |

## 90. What did they say? Berichten Sie in indirekter Rede!

a. *The weather forecast predicted: "Temperatures will rise."*

_______________________________________________

b. *The news reader reported: "Unemployment figures have dropped."*

_______________________________________________

c. *My mother always told me: "Wash your hands before dinner."*

_______________________________________________

d. *The doctor advised me: "Stay in bed for a few days!"*

_______________________________________________

e. *My neighbours asked me: "Could you babysit for us tonight?"*

_______________________________________________

f. *I asked her: "How old are you?"*

_______________________________________________

g. *Eve and Adam announced: "We are getting married next month."*

_______________________________________________

Lösung 91: a. break b. canteen c. sandwich d. selection e. corner f. serve g. side h. cheese i. pot j. coffee, cake k. fish l. hot m. burger, shake n. course o. wine

Lösung 90: a. The weather forecast predicted that temperatures would rise. b. The news reader reported that unemployment figures had dropped. c. My mother always told me to wash my hands before dinner. d. The doctor advised me to stay in bed for a few days. e. My neighbours asked me to babysit for them tonight. / My neighbours asked me if I could babysit for them tonight. f. I asked her how old she was. g. Eve and Adam announced that they were getting married next month.

## 91. Feeling Hungry? Wie wär's mit einem Imbiss?

| | |
|---|---|
| a. *Isn't it time for our lunch _ _ _ _ _?* | **serve** |
| b. *O.K , let's go to the _ _ _ _ _!* | **course** |
| c. *I'll just have a cheese and ham _ _ _ _ _ and a soft drink.* | **burger, shake** |
| d. *The sandwich bar across the road has a good _ _ _ _ _.* | **coffee, cake** |
| e. *They also do lunch at the pub around the _ _ _ _ _.* | **cheese** |
| f. *I think you have to _ _ _ _ _ yourself at the buffet.* | **pot** |
| g. *I'd like a baked potato with a _ _ _ _ _ salad.* | **corner** |
| h. *I think I'll have a _ _ _ _ _ and coleslaw roll and a cup of tea.* | **break** |
| i. *A _ _ _ _ _ of tea for two, please!* | **canteen** |
| j. *Let's have a cup of _ _ _ _ _ and a slice of _ _ _ _ _ in that little café over there.* | **sandwich** |
| k. *How about _ _ _ _ _ and chips for dinner? I'll get them at the take away.* | **selection** |
| l. *There's a stand outside the station where you can get excellent _ _ _ _ _ dogs.* | **hot** |
| m. *I'm in a hurry. I'll just get a _ _ _ _ _ and a milk _ _ _ _ _ at the drive-in.* | **wine** |
| n. *I love having big five _ _ _ _ _ dinners in fancy restaurants.* | **fish** |
| o. *I really enjoy having some Italian pasta dish and a glas of red _ _ _ _ _.* | **side** |

## 92. Give & Take Setzen Sie die passenden Ausdrücke in Ihrer richtigen Form ein!

| | | |
|---|---|---|
| a. | His hobby <u>occupies</u> all his leisure time. → ______ | give or take |
| b. | Are you willing to <u>undertake</u> this job? → ______ | take on |
| c. | We have to <u>consider</u> all the pros and cons of this idea. → ______ | take up |
| d. | Did I tell you that they will <u>give me the job</u>? → ______ | give in |
| e. | I think you really should <u>have a day's holiday</u>. → ______ | give away |
| f. | We all enjoyed the ride, <u>except perhaps</u> a few people. → ______ | take into account |
| g. | I am not going to <u>yield</u> to all this pressure. → ______ | take me on |
| h. | She gets upset when people <u>don't appreciate</u> her. → ______ | take a day off |
| i. | It's not my fault. You shouldn't <u>get angry with</u> me. → ______ | take it out on |
| j. | He should <u>give consideration</u> to our feelings. → ______ | take account of |
| k. | I need some exercise. I should <u>start</u> jogging again. → ______ | take up |
| l. | Smoking is so bad for your health. You have to <u>stop</u>. → ______ | take for granted |
| m. | <u>Dismantle</u> it if you know how to reassemble it. → ______ | take part |
| n. | <u>Revealing</u> the secret led to unpleasant reactions. → ______ | take apart |
| o. | Would you like to <u>participate</u> in this game? → ______ | give it up |

Lösung 93: a. themselves b. — c. yourself d. herself e. ourselves f. — g. herself h. — i. — j. itself k. — l. yourself m. — n. ourselves o. —

Lösung 92: a. takes up b. take it on c. take into account d. take me on e. take a day off f. give or take g. give in h. take her for granted i. take it out on j. take account of k. take up l. give it up m. Take it apart n. Giving away o. take part

## 93. How selfish! Ergänzen Sie das Reflexivpronomen wenn nötig!

a. *I hope they enjoyed ______ at the party.*
b. *Please hurry ______!*
c. *You can only blame ______ for what you've done.*
d. *She spent hours looking at ______ in the mirror.*
e. *It's alright, we can pay for ______.*
f. *He got up and washed and shaved ______.*
g. *She got out of the shower and dried ______ with a towel.*
h. *She is sitting ______ down on the chair.*
i. *Don't worry ______!*
j. *The film ______ wasn't very good. But I liked the music.*
k. *I tried to study but I just couldn't concentrate ______.*
l. *If somebody attacks you, you need to be able to defend ______.*
m. *John and I will meet ______ outside the pub at 8.30.*
n. *We couldn't get back into the house because we had locked ______ out.*
o. *Why don't you sit down and relax ______ for a while.*

## 94. Must, Should & Need Wie muss es heißen?

| | | |
|---|---|---|
| a. | *We really _ _ _ _ _ run if we want to catch this train.* | **must** |
| b. | *We've got plenty of time. We _ _ _ _ _ hurry.* | **mustn't** |
| c. | *Didn't you say I _ _ _ _ _ bring an umbrella?* | **should** |
| d. | *But I _ _ _ _ _ have brought it at all. It didn't rain all day.* | **needn't** |
| e. | *We _ _ _ _ _ forget to post that letter that Jim gave us.* | **need** |
| f. | *Do we need any groceries? _ _ _ _ _ we go to the supermarket?* | **needn't** |
| g. | *We still have enough food at home. We _ _ _ _ _ go shopping today.* | **must** |
| h. | *_ _ _ _ _ I take one of your bags?* | **mustn't** |
| i. | *No, you _ _ _ _ _ help me. They aren't very heavy.* | **should** |
| j. | *I have to tell you a secret but you _ _ _ _ _ tell anyone!* | **should** |
| k. | *If it's the story about Jean you _ _ _ _ _ tell me, because I know it already.* | **needn't** |
| l. | *Oh, you _ _ _ _ _ have told me that you know about it, too!* | **needn't** |
| m. | *So do you think we _ _ _ _ _ do something about it?* | **should** |
| n. | *I think we really _ _ _ _ _ to discuss this with Jean personally.* | **needn't** |
| o. | *Yes, we definitely _ _ _ _ _ talk to her.* | **should** |

Lösung 95: g - c - f - e - b - a - o - m - d - j - h - i - l - k - n

Lösung 94: a. must b. needn't c. should d. needn't e. mustn't f. Should g. needn't h. Should i. needn't j. mustn't k. needn't l. should m. should n. need o. must

## 95. Too busy! Bringen Sie das Telefongespräch in die richtige Reihenfolge!

a. *Packing? Where are you going?*
b. *I'm packing.*
c. *Ellen, hello. It's Liz. How are you?*
d. *No, we're going to Paris for a long weekend.*
e. *Why? What are you doing?*
f. *I'm fine but very busy!*
g. *375 6849. Hello?*
h. *We're moving upstairs to a bigger flat.*
i. *Ah, I see. Listen Ellen, I'm phoning because I'd like to invite you for dinner tonight.*
j. *But where are you moving then?*
k. *Well, maybe next time!*
l. *Oh, I'm sorry, I think we're too busy. But thanks for the invitation.*
m. *What? You're moving to Paris?*
n. *Yes, and you also have to come over to our new place some time!*
o. *Well, tomorrow we're flying to Paris and in three weeks we're moving.*

## 96. Suggestions & Advices Wie lauten die Sätze?

a. me a to suggestion make allow

b. this considered you possibility have

c. to advise over think I it you

d. do you situation in what my would

e. advice you to your ask like I'd for

f. do way rather this wouldn't it you

g. have you suggestions don't better any

Lösung 97: a. call ... back b. think ... over c. talk ... into d. speak up e. call off f. put ... off g. look after h. speak out i. talk down j. call out k. call ... up l. look up m. Look out n. look for

Lösung 96: a. Allow me to make a suggestion. b. Have you considered this possibility? c. I advise you to think it over. d. What would you do in my situation? e. I'd like to ask you for your advice. f. Wouldn't you rather do it this way? g. Don't you have any better suggestion?

## 97. SAY IT RIGHT! Wie muss es heißen?

a. *I should know the answer tomorrow, can you ___ me ___ then?*
b. *I can't make up my mind right away. I'll need to ___ it ___.*
c. *I know she doesn't want to do it, but I'll try to ___ her ___ helping us.*
d. *I'm afraid I can't hear you very well, could you ___, please?*
e. *We'll have to ___ the lecture ___ because the speaker is ill.*
f. *Can we ___ the meeting ___ to next Wednesday?*
g. *I promised them to ___ their garden while they are away.*
h. *He was afraid to ___ at the meeting in case he made a fool of himself.*
i. *It's very annoying when people ___ you ___ because they think they know it better.*
j. *Sometimes I want to ___ loud: "Leave me alone."*
k. *I always ___ my brother ___ on his birthday.*
l. *I have a lot of respect for this man. I really ___ to him.*
m. *___ for the big holes in the road!*
n. *I don't know where I put the keys. Can you please help me to ___ them?*

**call out**
**call off**
**call up**
**call back**
**put off**
**speak up**
**speak out**
**look up**
**look out**
**look for**
**look after**
**talk down**
**talk into**
**think over**

## 98. Hopes & Concerns Wie lauten die Sätze?

a. best for am I the hoping

b. on set you hopes have my I all

c. still of ray there hope a is

d. everything alright hope is I

e. you concerned really I about am

f. too worry not do much

g. about am it anxious I very

Lösung 99: a. say b. speak their minds c. on speaking terms d. It goes without saying e. You can say that again. f. talking point g. speak my mind h. think it over i. doesn't think much of j. it is no sooner said than done. k. I called his bluff. l. thought better of it. m. was thinking aloud.

Lösung 98: a. I am hoping for the best. b. I have set all my hopes on you. c. There still is a ray of hope. d. I hope everything is alright e. I am really concerned about you. f. Do not worry too much! g. I am very anxious about it.

## 99. PHRASES Ersetzen Sie das Unterstrichene mit einem der Ausdrücke!

a. *I'll start pouring out the wine - please tell me when to stop pouring.*
b. *When two business people meet, they often discuss work or business.*
c. *They had an argument and now they are not on friendly terms.*
d. *It's obvious that it takes time to get used to an unfamiliar accent.*
e. *"It's terrible, isn't it?" "I agree with you entirely."*
f. *Paul and his sheep are not a favourite discussion topic.*
g. *Unfortunately where I work I'm not able to express my views frankly.*
h. *It was a great idea at the time but could you ask Kevin to reconsider.*
i. *You can tell from his voice that he has a low opinion of your work.*
j. *Email is very fast indeed, it can be done quickly.*
k. *I didn't think he had the guts to do that, so I challenged him to go through with it.*
l. *We were going to take a canal barge but then decided it wasn't a good idea.*
m. *Don't take Geraldine too seriously, she was just saying her thoughts out loud.*

**say**
**on speaking terms**
**talking point**
**it is no sooner said than done**
**speak one's mind**
**think aloud**
**not think much of**
**it goes without saying**
**think it over**
**you can say that again**
**speak one's mind**
**think better of it**
**call one's bluff**

## 100. Going on Holidays Ergänzen Sie den Dialog mit der richtigen Verbform!

a. *So you (go) ______ to England tomorrow?*
b. *Yes, by this time tomorrow, we (be) ______ on our way.*
c. *(you/fly) ______ from Hamburg?*
d. *No, we (not/go) ______ by air this time.*
e. *We (travel) ______ to Ostende by train and then (take) ______ the ferry to Dover.*
f. *What time (be) ______ your train?*
g. *Well, there's one that (leave) ______ at 5.30.*
h. *That's very early. The first bus (not/go) ______ till 5.35, you know.*
i. *No? Oh, then we (take) ______ a taxi to the station.*
j. *So tomorrow you (have) ______ lunch somewhere in mid-channel.*
k. *That's right. I hope it (not/be) ______ too rough.*
l. *Don't worry. I'm sure the weather (stay) ______ fine.*
m. *Well, I (hope) ______ so.*
n. *(have) ______ a good time!*
o. *Thanks. We (send) ______ you a postcard!*

Lösung 101: a. I have to get my passport renewed b. I have to get 4 photographs taken. c. I have to get the car washed. d. I have to get the oil changed e. I have to get the tyre pressure checked. f. I have to get the radio repaired. g. I have to get vaccinated. h. I have to get the films developed. i. I have to get my dress altered. j. I have to get these shoes mended. k. I have to get my hair cut. l. I have to get money changed. m. I have to get the flowers watered. n. I have to get the cat fed.

Lösung 100: a. are going b. will be c. Will you be flying d. won't go e. are travelling, take f. is g. leaves h. won't go i. will take j. will be having k. won't be l. will stay m. hope n. Have o. will send

## 101. Get things done Erzählen Sie, was Sie vor dem Urlaub erledigen müssen!

a. *renew passport* ______________________________.
b. *take 4 photographs* ______________________________.
c. *wash car* ______________________________.
d. *change oil* ______________________________.
e. *check tyre pressure* ______________________________.
f. *repair radio* ______________________________.
g. *vaccinate* ______________________________.
h. *develop films* ______________________________.
i. *alter dress* ______________________________.
j. *mend shoes* ______________________________.
k. *cut hair* ______________________________.
l. *change money* ______________________________.
m. *water flowers* ______________________________.
n. *feed cat* ______________________________.

## 102. WHERE TO STAY? Füllen Sie die Lücken!

| | |
|---|---|
| a. *Could you _ _ _ _ a good hotel around here?* | **only** |
| b. *Joyce's Hotel is the _ _ _ _ in town.* | **around** |
| c. *How much does it _ _ _ _ per night?* | **know** |
| d. *70 pounds for a _ _ _ _ room en suite.* | **expensive** |
| e. *And which meals are _ _ _ _?* | **included** |
| f. *Only breakfast. Lunch and dinner are _ _ _ _.* | **sounds** |
| g. *That's a little bit too _ _ _ _ for us.* | **best** |
| h. *Wouldn't you _ _ _ _ anything cheaper?* | **recommend** |
| i. *Well, you could _ _ _ _ in a B&B.* | **continental** |
| j. *I know a very good one, and it's just _ _ _ _ the corner.* | **extra** |
| k. *Could we have a _ _ _ _ there?* | **consists** |
| l. *No, they _ _ _ _ do breakfast. But it's a big Irish breakfast.* | **full board** |
| m. *What's that? I only know _ _ _ _ breakfast.* | **double** |
| n. *An Irish breakfast is very rich. It _ _ _ _ of eggs, bacon, and saussages.* | **stay** |
| o. *That _ _ _ _ good. I think we'll go for it.* | **cost** |

Lösung 103: a. 13 b. 10 c. 12 d. 11 e. 8 f. 7 g. 4 h. 3 i. 2 j. 1 k. 6 l. 9 m. 5

Lösung 102: a. recommend b. best c. cost d. double e. included f. extra g. expensive h. know i. stay j. around k. full board l. only m. continental n. consists o. sounds

## 103. Booking into a Hotel

Welche Antwort passt zu welcher Frage?

a. *Do you have any vacancies for tonight?*
b. *Could I have a room with a view?*
c. *Would you like a double room?*
d. *Do you have any identification with you?*
e. *Is there a lift?*
f. *How many nights would you like to stay?*
g. *Can I see the room please?*
h. *Could someone help me with my bags?*
i. *And which meals are included?*
j. *Is that with or without bathroom?*
k. *Could I have a wake up call?*
l. *When can I have breakfast?*
m. *Can I make outside calls?*

1. *All our rooms are en suite.*
2. *Only breakfast. Dinner is extra.*
3. *Of course. I'll call the porter.*
4. *Yes, let me show you the way.*
5. *Yes, but you have to dial '0' first.*
6. *At what time would you like it?*
7. *Just the one.*
8. *I'm afraid it's broken at the moment.*
9. *It's served from 7 a.m. until 10.30 a.m.*
10. *This one overlooks the park.*
11. *Yes, here's my passport.*
12. *No, two singles please.*
13. *Yes, but only on the top floor.*

## 104. Checking in! Füllen Sie die Lücken!

| | |
|---|---|
| a. Hello, do you have any _ _ _ _ _ _? | **dining room** |
| b. Hello, my name is Brown and I have a _ _ _ _ _ _. | **room service** |
| c. Would you like an _ _ _ _ _ _ shower? | **single** |
| d. Was the room paid for in _ _ _ _ _ _ or by credit card? | **mini-bar** |
| e. Our _ _ _ _ _ _ is on the very top floor. | **en suite** |
| f. A _ _ _ _ _ _ will grab your luggage for you, madam. | **safe** |
| g. What number do we dial for _ _ _ _ _ _? | **chambermaid** |
| h. What time does the _ _ _ _ _ _ come by at? | **reservation** |
| i. You're joking! You actually have a vegetarian _ _ _ _ _ _ _ _ _ _ _ _?!? | **entertainment** |
| j. Before 8 p.m., all starters are _ _ _ _ _ _. | **twin** |
| k. Did you see that the _ _ _ _ _ _ wasn't charged to our bill? | **porter** |
| l. I believe there's an _ _ _ _ _ _ programme that starts about 9 p.m. | **complimentary** |
| m. Excuse me, I was looking for two _ _ _ _ _ _ rooms. | **vacancies** |
| n. We have a double room with _ _ _ _ _ _ beds available. | **suite** |
| o. Do you have a _ _ _ _ _ _ where I can leave my valuables? | **cash** |

Lösung 105: d - c - f - o - a - e - l - g - k - m - j - h - b - i

Lösung 104: a. vacancies b. reservation c. en suite d. cash e. suite f. porter g. room service h. chambermaid i. dining room j. complimentary k. mini-bar l. entertainment m. single n. twin o. safe

## 105. Complaints Bringen Sie den Dialog in die richtige Reihenfolge!

a. *Is everything else in order?*
b. *Certainly, sir. Good night.*
c. *Yes, sir. How can I help you?*
d. *Hello, reception. This is room 24.*
e. *Actually, it isn't. Our TV doesn't seem to be working.*
f. *I'm afraid that there are no towels in our bathroom.*
g. *That's great. Thank you very much.*
h. *Ok, seven o'clock. Could you please give me a wake-up call at 6.30 then?*
i. *Good night.*
j. *It's served between 7 o'clock and 10.30.*
k. *Anything else I can do for you, sir?*
l. *I'm terribly sorry, sir. We'll get you another one immediately.*
m. *Yes, could you please tell me what time breakfast is being served.*
o. *I'm very sorry. I'll have some brought to you immediately.*

## 106. Eating out? Was passt in die Lücken?

a. *Shall we go out for ____ somewhere?*
b. *Oh yes, I'd ____ to.*
c. *Where shall we go? Any ____?*
d. *A colleague ____ this new Japanese place to me.*
e. *I'm not too ____ on Japanese cuisine with all the raw fish.*
f. *O.K. Let's go somewhere ____ then.*
g. *What about Beshoffs restaurant? They have nice ____ food there.*
h. *We go there all the ____, I'd like to try something new.*
i. *Alright. What would you ____ then?*
j. *I'd love some Italian ____.*
k. *____ don't we go to the Italian in Dorset Street then.*
l. *It's always packed there. You don't get a table unless you ____ a day in advance.*
m. *You know what? Why don't we just ____ a pizza and stay in then?*
n. *The take- ____ around the corner has a nice selection.*
o. *Sound's good. Let's stay at ____ and get a video as well then.*

***recommended***
***home***
***suggestions***
***food***
***reserve***
***dinner***
***order***
***love***
***time***
***keen***
***else***
***traditional***
***like***
***why***
***away***

Lösung 107: g - e - b - f - n - c - i - h - j - a - o - d - m - l - k

Lösung 106: a. dinner b. love c. suggestions d. recommended e. keen f. else g. traditional h. time i. like j. food k. why l. reserve m. order n. away o. home

## 107. Can I take your Order? Bringen Sie den Dialog in die richtige Reihenfolge!

a. *And as a side dish?*
b. *Thank you very much.*
c. *May I take your order now?*
d. *Fine, what would you like to drink?*
e. *Would you come this way please. Take a seat, here's the menu.*
f. *Are you ready to order?*
g. *Good evening. I've booked a table under the name of Jones.*
h. *And for main course?*
i. *Yes, we'll start with the soup of the day.*
j. *I'll have the salmon and my husband will have the sirloin steak.*
k. *That sounds good. We'll try it.*
l. *I can offer you a 1987 vintage.*
m. *We'll take a bottle of Chardonnay, please.*
n. *No, we haven't decided yet.*
o. *We'll have a green salad and baked potatoes.*

## 108. At a Chinese Restaurant   Wie muss es heißen?

| | |
|---|---|
| a. *What are you _ _ _ _ _ ?* | **problem** |
| b. *I think I'll _ _ _ _ _ for the roast duck in plum sauce.* | **live** |
| c. *That _ _ _ _ _ good.* | **fortune** |
| d. *And _ _ _ _ _ are you having?* | **won't** |
| e. *I _ _ _ _ _ I'll have the sweet and sour pork.* | **some** |
| f. *But you had that the _ _ _ _ _ time!* | **last** |
| g. *Don't you want to try _ _ _ _ _ new?* | **think** |
| h. *I'll have _ _ _ _ _ of your duck.* | **new** |
| i. *No, you _ _ _ _ _.* | **sounds** |
| j. *OK, then I'll have the duck, _ _ _ _ _.* | **having** |
| k. *What does your _ _ _ _ _ cookie say?* | **go** |
| l. *It says: "You will _ _ _ _ _ a long happy life with your wife."* | **what** |
| m. *I think we've got a _ _ _ _ _.* | **anything** |
| n. *Why? What does _ _ _ _ _ say?* | **too** |
| o. *Mine says: "You will find _ _ _ _ _ love with a tall and handsome man."* | **yours** |

Lösung 109: a. 9 b. 3 c. 11 d. 1 e. 6 f. 5 g. 13 h. 2 i. 8 j. 4 k. 10 l. 14 m. 12 n. 7

Lösung 108: a. having b. go c. sounds d. what e. think f. last g. anything h. some i. won't j. too k. fortune l. live m. problem n. yours o. new

## 109. Eating at Home

Welche Sätze passen am besten zusammen?

a. *Dinner's ready!*
b. *Do you want me to lay the table?*
c. *Where shall I sit?*
d. *Can you hand me the butter, please?*
e. *Would you like some ham?*
f. *Can I have some more peas please?*
g. *Did you enjoy the meal?*
h. *What about some dessert?*
i. *What's for dessert?*
j. *Can't I tempt you?*
k. *Would you like tea or coffee?*
l. *How do you take your tea?*
m. *Here you are.*
n. *Can I help you with the dishes?*

1. *Of course, here you go.*
2. *No, thanks. I just couldn't eat any more!*
3. *No, thank you. It's already set.*
4. *Well, if you insist.*
5. *Please help yourself!*
6. *No thanks. I'm a vegetarian.*
7. *There's no need to. I have a dishwasher.*
8. *I have fruit or ice cream.*
9. *I'm coming. It smells delicious!*
10. *I'd love a cup of tea.*
11. *Anywhere you like.*
12. *Oh, lovely. Thanks.*
13. *Yes, very much so. It was delicious.*
14. *With milk and two sugars, please.*

## 110. A Tourist in New York

Ergänzen Sie die fehlenden Wörter!

| | |
|---|---|
| a. Excuse me, where's the Tourist Information _ _ _ _? | much |
| b. Sorry, I'm not _ _ _ _ here. | welcome |
| c. I see. Thank's _ _ _ _. | block |
| d. Excuse me, can you _ _ _ _ me where the Tourist Information Center is? | change |
| e. It's on 42nd Street, _ _ _ _ Times Square. Have you got a _ _ _ _? | line |
| f. Yes, here it is. Let's take a _ _ _ _. | off |
| g. OK, we're on Pearl Street. You go _ _ _ _ Pearl Street and turn right. | tell |
| h. That's Grand Street. The subway _ _ _ _ is on the left. | from |
| i. Which _ _ _ _ do I take? | Center |
| j. You take the B, D or Q train going _ _ _ _, it's the orange line. | anyway |
| k. _ _ at Washington Square and take the A, C or E train, that's the blue line. | near, map |
| l. You get _ _ _ _ at 42nd Street. | look |
| m. The Tourist Information Center is one _ _ _ _ east of the station. | down |
| n. Thank you very _ _ _ _. | station |
| o. You're _ _ _ _. | uptown |

Lösung 111: a. Where b. How c. what d. lost e. left f. station g. bus h. taxi i. foot j. crossroads k. Could l. tourist m. direction n. map o. policeman

Lösung 110: a. Center b. from c. anyway d. tell e. near, map f. look g. down h. station i. line j. uptown k. Change l. off m. block n. much o. welcome

## 111. GET LOST! Welche Wörter gehören in die Lücken?

| | |
|---|---|
| a. _ _ _ _ is the nearest cinema? | station |
| b. _ _ _ _ far is it to the next bus stop? | policeman |
| c. Excuse me, but _ _ _ _ is the name of this street? | bus |
| d. Hello, I think that I am _ _ _ _! | where |
| e. It is the first one-way street on the _ _ _ _. | map |
| f. Your hotel is next to the train _ _ _ _. | direction |
| g. If you go around the next corner, the _ _ _ _ station is straight ahead. | could |
| h. Where is the nearest _ _ _ _ rank? | tourist |
| i. How far is the gallery on _ _ _ _? | how |
| j. You continue through the _ _ _ _ and Bow Street is on your right. | lost |
| k. _ _ _ _ you show me the way to the museum on the map, please? | left |
| l. Sorry, I'm a _ _ _ _ here myself! | what |
| m. Oh, I'm afraid you're going in the wrong _ _ _ _ completely! | taxi |
| n. Could you show me on the _ _ _ _, please? | foot |
| o. Maybe you should ask that _ _ _ _ for directions. | crossroads |

## 112. Buying a Train Ticket

Bringen Sie den Dialog in die richtige Reihenfolge!

a. *How much does a seat in first class cost?*
b. *Non-smoking, please.*
c. *And in first class?*
d. *4.35 this afternoon.*
e. *I'd like to buy a return ticket to Edinburgh, please.*
f. *Smoking or non-smoking?*
g. *I'm afraid we don't have any non-smoking seats left on this train.*
h. *How can I help you, madam?*
i. *O.K. I'll take first class then. Which platform does the train leave from?*
j. *Thank you. Enjoy your trip.*
k. *That would be 100 pounds plus the 4 pounds supplement.*
l. *From platform twelve. That'll be 104 pounds altogether then.*
m. *For what time?*
n. *Yes, there are two non-smokers' seats left in first class.*
o. *Here you are.*

Lösung 113: a. seat b. free c. back d. open e. quite f. stops g. sure h. conductor i. Tickets j. supplement k. pounds l. now m. just n. long o. too

Lösung 112: h - e - m - d - f - b - g - c - n - a - k - i - l - o - j

## 113. On the Train Welche Wörter passen in die Lücken?

| | | |
|---|---|---|
| a. | *Excuse me, is this _ _ _ _ taken?* | **long** |
| b. | *No, it's _ _ _ _.* | **pounds** |
| c. | *I can't travel with my _ _ _ _ to the engine. I better sit down there.* | **conductor** |
| d. | *It's very warm in here. May I _ _ _ _ a window?* | **stops** |
| e. | *Please do. It's _ _ _ _ stuffy, isn't it?* | **open** |
| f. | *Do you know how many _ _ _ _ there are 'til Heuston Station?* | **too** |
| g. | *I'm not quite _ _ _ _. Five, I think.* | **back** |
| h. | *Oh, here's the _ _ _ _. Where did I put my ticket?* | **free** |
| i. | *_ _ _ _ please!* | **seat** |
| j. | *Can I pay the _ _ _ _ now?* | **quite** |
| k. | *Yes, it's four _ _ _ _ please.* | **sure** |
| l. | *Where are we _ _ _ _?* | **tickets** |
| m. | *We are _ _ _ _ outside London.* | **supplement** |
| n. | *How _ _ _ _ do we stop for?* | **now** |
| o. | *Not for _ _ _ _ long. Approximately 5 minutes.* | **just** |

## 114. Catch a Bus

Welche Wörter gehören in die Lücken?

a. *Could you please tell me where the ____ bus stop is?*
b. *It's just ____ the corner there. You can't miss it.*
c. *Excuse me, please. ____ bus do I take to Fairview Park?*
d. *You have to take ____ 32.*
e. *It ____ be here in two or three minutes.*
f. *A single ____ to Mountjoy Square please.*
g. *____ twenty five please.*
h. *Could you please tell me ____ we get there please?*
i. *You have to get ____ the next stop.*
j. *Is this the ____ for the city centre?*
k. *No. you're going the ____ direction.*
l. *You should have ____ a 67A.*
m. *Get off the ____ stop and take the next bus going west.*
n. *Buses run from there ____ fifteen minutes.*
o. *It seems the bus is ____ a few minutes late.*

**every**
**ticket**
**next**
**should**
**number**
**which**
**around**
**nearest**
**running**
**when**
**one**
**off**
**bus**
**wrong**
**caught**

Lösung 115: a. Where can I exchange some money? b. Where is the nearest bureau de change? c. What is the rate of exchange? d. How much do I get for 100 DM? e. I would like to cash this traveller's cheque. f. Is there a cash dispenser near here? g. Could I also have some small change?

Lösung 114: a. nearest b. around c. Which d. number e. should f. ticket g. One h. when i. off j. bus k. wrong l. caught m. next n. every o. running

## 115. At the Bank

Formen Sie sinnvolle Sätze!

a. I | exchange | where | money | some | can

b. the | is | bureau de change | nearest | where

c. of | rate | is | exchange | what | the

d. do | get | 100 DM | much | I | how | for

e. to | traveller's | this | cash | would | like | I | cheque

f. cash | there | is | near | dispenser | a | here

g. have | change | I | some | small | could | also

## 116. BANKING TERMS Welche Definition ist die richtige?

a. *bank counter*

1. money token issued by the bank
2. desk at which bank business is done
3. teller in a bank

b. *interests*

1. how to invest your money
2. what people do with their money
3. sum paid for borrowed money

c. *payee*

1. bank client
2. recipient of payment
3. person paying money to the bank

d. *mortgage*

1. security for a personal loan
2. interest payable on property
3. loan secured by property

e. *account*

1. person´s money held in bank
2. certain quantity of money
3. money lend to someone by the bank

f. *PIN number*

1. number of the account
2. number printed on cheque card
3. code for automated teller machines

Lösung 117: a. post b. parcel c. weigh d. stamps e. special-issue f. take g. surface h. labels i. register j. withdraw k. letters l. forwarded m. words n. postal o. customs

Lösung 116: a. 2 b. 3 c. 2 d. 3 e. 1 f. 3

## 117. Post for me! Was passt in die Lücken?

a. *I'd like to _ _ _ _ these letters to the United States, please.*
b. *How much does it cost to send a _ _ _ _ to Austria?*
c. *I'd have to _ _ _ _ it first.*
d. *I'd like two 40 pence _ _ _ _.*
e. *Do you have any _ _ _ _ stamps?*
f. *How long does a letter to Australia _ _ _ _?*
g. *It depends. Airmail or _ _ _ _ mail?*
h. *Can I have half a dozen airmail _ _ _ _ and a book of stamps, please?*
i. *I'd like to _ _ _ _ this letter and send it by express.*
j. *Can I _ _ _ _ money from my post office savings book?*
k. *Are there any _ _ _ _ for me?*
l. *I would like to have my mail _ _ _ _ to this address.*
m. *I'd like to send a telegram. How much do ten _ _ _ _ cost?*
n. *Could I make a _ _ _ _ order, please?*
o. *You'll have to fill out this _ _ _ _ form first.*

**labels**
**stamps**
**weigh**
**post**
**parcel**
**special-issue**
**customs**
**postal**
**words**
**forwarded**
**letters**
**withdraw**
**register**
**surface**
**take**

## 118. Going to the Movies

Füllen Sie die Lücken!

a. *Would you like to go to the _ _ _ _ _ _ tonight?*
b. *Which _ _ _ _ _ _ should we see?*
c. *I don't know. Let's check the _ _ _ _ _ _.*
d. *I saw a _ _ _ _ _ _ for this one, it should be good.*
e. *Yes, it had good _ _ _ _ _ _, too.*
f. *What _ _ _ _ _ _ are in this film?*
g. *I don't know but it was made by a famous _ _ _ _ _ _.*
h. *What _ _ _ _ _ _ does the movie have?*
i. *It says _ _ _ _ _ _.*
j. *What time does the _ _ _ _ _ _ start.*
k. *At eight. Do you think we can still get _ _ _ _ _ _?*
l. *We should definitely _ _ _ _ _ _ in advance.*
m. *I can pay by _ _ _ _ _ _.*
n. *We have to collect our tickets from the _ _ _ _ _ _.*
o. *Let's get a big bowl of _ _ _ _ _ _!*

***box office***
***trailer***
***cinema***
***director***
***parental guidance***
***tickets***
***popcorn***
***credit card***
***film***
***book***
***reviews***
***certificate***
***actors***
***program***
***paper***

Lösung 119: a. Are there still tickets available? b. Yes, but only in the rear stalls. c. Are there any balcony seats left? d. I'm afraid it's completely sold out e. I'd like a seat in one of the boxes. f. There is only standing room g. Do you have a seating plan?

Lösung 118: a. cinema b. film c. paper d. trailer e. reviews f. actors g. director h. certificate i. parental guidance j. program k. tickets l. book m. credit card n. box office o. popcorn

## 119. Booking a Ticket Bilden Sie Sätze!

a. still available there tickets are

b. stalls but the in only yes rear

c. seats there any are left balcony

d. out it's afraid sold I'm completely

e. one boxes like I'd a seat of in the

f. room only is there standing

g. have plan you seating do a

## 120. At the Theatre Welche Wörter sind gesucht?

| | |
|---|---|
| a. Shall we buy a _ _ _ _ _? | supporting |
| b. I would like to get rid of my _ _ _ _ _ first. | performance |
| c. The _ _ _ _ _ is over there. Where are we sitting? | opera-glass |
| d. Let's have a look at the _ _ _ _ _. | stairs |
| e. On the second balcony, first _ _ _ _ _, seats 3 and 4. | balcony |
| f. Excuse me, sir! Can you show us how to get to the _ _ _ _ _? | tickets |
| g. Yes, certainly, madam. Take the _ _ _ _ _ here on your right. | subscription |
| h. Wow, we're so high up. The _ _ _ _ _ looks tiny from here. | cloakroom |
| i. I told you we should have brought your mother's _ _ _ _ _! | program |
| j. Ssh! They are raising the _ _ _ _ _. It must be starting.... | coat |
| k. Well, how did you enjoy the _ _ _ _ _? | row |
| l. The set was wonderful and I was very impressed by the _ _ _ _ _. | stage |
| m. The main actor was great, but the _ _ _ _ _ actress stole the show. | curtain |
| n. We definitely have to go to the theatre more _ _ _ _ _! | acting |
| o. Why don't we take out a _ _ _ _ _ for the next season? | often |

Lösung 121: a. 6 b. 13 c. 11 d. 9 e. 8 f. 2 g. 1 h. 12 i. 10 j. 4 k. 5 l. 14 m. 15 n. 7 o. 3

Lösung 120: a. program b. coat c. cloakroom d. tickets e. row f. balcony g. stairs h. stage i. opera-glass j. curtain k. performance l. acting m. supporting n. often o. subscription

## 121. See the Doctor! Welche Satzhälften gehören zusammen?

| | |
|---|---|
| a. *What time does the doctor …* | 1. *… be the trouble?* |
| b. *I can give you an appointment …* | 2. *… longer than ten minutes.* |
| c. *Could you please fill in this …* | 3. *… five days if you don't feel any better.* |
| d. *I've come for my …* | 4. *… mouth and say "ah".* |
| e. *Could you take a seat in …* | 5. *… prescription for some antibiotics.* |
| f. *It shouldn't be …* | 6. *… have her consulting hour?* |
| g. *What seems to …* | 7. *… me a doctor's certificate, please?* |
| h. *I think I'm going …* | 8. *… the waiting room, please?* |
| i. *I haven't felt …* | 9. *… six o'clock appointment.* |
| j. *Please open your …* | 10. *… well for some days.* |
| k. *I'll make you out a …* | 11. *… form while you are waiting?* |
| l. *Please take two …* | 12. *… down on something.* |
| m. *You'll have to stay in …* | 13. *… for six o'clock this evening.* |
| n. *Could you give …* | 14. *… tablets three times a day.* |
| o. *Come back and see me again in …* | 15. *… bed for a few days.* |

## 122. The Doctor's Advice

Wie heißen die korrekten Hilfsverben?

a. *You shouldn't ______ waited so long.*
b. *You ______ better come to me earlier.*
c. *You ______ supposed to let me know if it got worse, weren't you?*
d. *You ______ to take better care of yourself.*
e. *First of all you ______ to give up smoking.*
f. *And regular exercise ______ do you any harm.*
g. *You ______ need to give up alcohol completely.*
h. *But you ______ drink more than a beer per day.*
i. *You ______ eat anything until it's not too much.*
j. *But you ______ eat more food than the body needs.*
k. *And you ______ give up those late night snacks.*
l. *You ______ eat more vitamins and minerals.*
m. *You ______ to cut down on crisps, chips and sweets.*
n. *This way you are going to ______ a healthy diet.*
o. *______ forget to come back in two weeks!*

Lösung 123: a. toothache b. mouth c. fillings d. temporary e. crowns f. remove g. care h. X-ray i. decayed j. numb k. drink l. infection m. antibiotics n. something o. prescription

Lösung 122: a. have b. had c. were d. have e. have/ought f. won't/wouldn't g. don't h. shouldn't i. can j. shouldn't k. must l. should m. have/ought n. have o. Don't

## 123. AT THE DENTIST Was passt in die Lücken?

a. *I've got a terrible _ _ _ _ _ _.*
b. *Please open your _ _ _ _ _ _ and I'll have a look.*
c. *You have bad cavities, you will need some _ _ _ _ _ _.*
d. *This is only a _ _ _ _ _ _ filling, I will put in the real one next week.*
e. *Would you prefer gold or porcelain _ _ _ _ _ _?*
f. *Shall I _ _ _ _ _ _ the tartar as well?*
g. *You must take better _ _ _ _ _ of your teeth and brush them regularly.*
h. *An _ _ _ _ _ _ will show if the root is all right.*
i. *Your wisdom teeth will have to come out, the roots are _ _ _ _ _ _.*
j. *This local anaesthetic will _ _ _ _ _ _ the whole area.*
k. *Please don't eat and _ _ _ _ _ _ for four hours.*
l. *You seem to have a gum _ _ _ _ _ _.*
m. *I will prescribe you some _ _ _ _ _ _ and a mouthwash.*
n. *Can you give me _ _ _ _ _ _ for the pain?*
o. *I'll give you a _ _ _ _ _ _ for some strong pain killers.*

**prescription**
**infection**
**drink**
**numb**
**decayed**
**care**
**crowns**
**fillings**
**toothache**
**mouth**
**something**
**temporary**
**remove**
**X-ray**
**antibiotics**

## 124. At the Police Station

Welche Antwort passt auf welche Frage?

a. *How can I help you?*
b. *What has been stolen?*
c. *When did this happen?*
d. *And where exactly did it happen?*
e. *What does it look like?*
f. *And what was in it?*
g. *Could I take down your personal details?*
h. *What's your name please?*
i. *Could you spell your surname?*
j. *What's your date of birth?*
k. *Where were you born?*
l. *What citizenship do you have?*
m. *What's your marital status?*
n. *What's your permanent address?*
o. *Officer, do you think I'll get it back?*

1. *It's brown leather and quite small.*
2. *Yes, of course.*
3. *Unfortunately the chances aren't very high.*
4. *In Liverpool.*
5. *My handbag.*
6. *I am British.*
7. *It's Gemma Bowden.*
8. *Today in the morning, around eleven.*
9. *I would like to report a theft.*
10. *It's 20 Marino Crescent, Dublin 3.*
11. *In the pedestrian zone in Henry Street.*
12. *My purse, a comb and some make-up.*
13. *B-O-W-D-E-N.*
14. *I'm single.*
15. *The second of March, 1971.*

Lösung 125: a. register b. municipal c. member d. permit e. purpose f. au pair g. planning h. least i. fill j. means k. support l. keeping m. process n. leaflet o. contact

Lösung 124: a. 9 b. 5 c. 8 d. 11 e. 1 f. 12 g. 2 h. 7 i. 13 j. 15 k. 4 l. 6 m. 14 n. 10 o. 3

## 125. Registration with the Authorities Setzen Sie ein!

a. *Do I have to _ _ _ _ with the authorities during my stay in this country?*
b. *You have to go to the _ _ _ _ office for registration.*
c. *Citizens belonging to a EU _ _ _ _ country have to report to room 134.*
d. *I've come to apply for a residence _ _ _ _.*
e. *What is the _ _ _ _ of your stay?*
f. *I want to work as an _ _ _ _ with a family here in London.*
g. *And how long are you _ _ _ _ to stay?*
h. *Probably one year, but at _ _ _ _ six months.*
i. *May I see your passport? And could you _ _ _ _ in this form, please?*
j. *Can you explain to me what it _ _ _ _ by question three on the form?*
k. *You must be able to prove that you have enough money to _ _ _ _ yourself.*
l. *How long will you be _ _ _ _ my passport?*
m. *It'll take about a week to _ _ _ _ your application.*
n. *Have you got a _ _ _ _ which explains the immigration laws in more detail?*
o. *We'll _ _ _ _ you by post when your papers are ready.*

**contact**
**process**
**support**
**leaflet**
**au pair**
**purpose**
**least**
**municipal**
**means**
**register**
**member**
**permit**
**planning**
**fill**
**keeping**

## 126. FLAT HUNT Bringen Sie das Gespräch in die richtige Reihenfolge!

a. *That's right. Could I come round some time and have a look at it?* ( )
b. *No. It's 80 pounds a week without heating or electricity.* ( )
c. *I see, that's in two weeks. Could you give me the exact address please.* ( )
d. *Ah, yes. Is it the one in Talbot Street that you are interested in?* ( )
e. *Yes, there is a deposit of 200 pounds to be payed in advance.* ( )
f. *And is the flat available immediately?* ( )
g. *Yes, the address is number 48, Talbot Street. And what's your name please?* ( )
h. *It will be free from the first of next month.* ( )
i. *Good, then Mr. Murray. See you at two tomorrow.* ( )
j. *Yes, two o'clock is fine for me. By the way, is electricity included in the rent?* ( )
k. *I see. That would be on top of the rent then. Do you require a deposit?* ( )
l. *Hello, I'm enquiring about your advertisement for the one-bedroom-flat.* ( )
m. *My name is Michael Murray.* ( )
n. *Would tomorrow afternoon suit you? Let's say around two o'clock?* ( )

Lösung 127: a. falsch (beat) b. falsch (matter) c. richtig d. falsch (smell) e. richtig f. falsch (red-handed) g. richtig h. richtig i. falsch (fire) j. richtig k. falsch (strike) l. richtig m. richtig n. falsch (done) o. falsch (horse's)

Lösung 126: l - d - a - n - j - b - k - e - f - h - c - g - m - i

## 127. Ideal Idioms? Welche Redewendungen sind falsch?

| | | | |
|---|---|---|---|
| a. | *Don't bear around the bush.* | richtig | falsch |
| b. | *It's master–of–course.* | richtig | falsch |
| c. | *make a beeline for* | richtig | falsch |
| d. | *I smack a rat!* | richtig | falsch |
| e. | *on the spur of the moment* | richtig | falsch |
| f. | *I was caught blue-handed.* | richtig | falsch |
| g. | *Let the cat out of the bag!* | richtig | falsch |
| h. | *out of the corner of my eye* | richtig | falsch |
| i. | *get on like a house on holidays* | richtig | falsch |
| j. | *when all is said and done* | richtig | falsch |
| k. | *stitch while the iron is hot* | richtig | falsch |
| l. | *pay through the nose* | richtig | falsch |
| m. | *keep an ear on the ground* | richtig | falsch |
| n. | *easier said than fun* | richtig | falsch |
| o. | *straight from the cow's mouth* | richtig | falsch |

## 128. Folk Wisdom Setzen Sie die richtigen Sprichwörter zusammen!

| | | | |
|---|---|---|---|
| a. | *An apple a day...* | ( ) | *... has a silver lining.* |
| b. | *He laughs best ...* | ( ) | *... who help themselves.* |
| c. | *People in glasshouses...* | ( ) | *... is worth two in the bush.* |
| d. | *Hunger is...* | ( ) | *... be choosers.* |
| e. | *God helps those...* | ( ) | *... make the most noise.* |
| f. | *In wine...* | ( ) | *... saves nine.* |
| g. | *One man's meat...* | ( ) | *... catches the worm.* |
| h. | *One should strike while...* | ( ) | *... the sun shines.* |
| i. | *Every cloud...* | ( ) | *... there is truth.* |
| j. | *The early bird...* | ( ) | *... who laughs last.* |
| k. | *Empty vessels...* | ( ) | *... shouldn't throw stones.* |
| l. | *A stitch in time...* | ( ) | *... is another man's poison.* |
| m. | *Make hay while...* | ( ) | *... the iron is hot.* |
| n. | *A bird in the hand...* | ( ) | *... keeps the doctor away.* |
| o. | *Beggars can't...* | ( ) | *... the best sauce.* |

Lösung 129: a. recount b. reconstruction c. reincarnation d. relive e. redo f. reposition g. replayed h. reproduction i. resit j. retrace k. reunion l. revamped m. remarry n. refuel

Lösung 128: a. An apple a day keeps the doctor away. b. He laughs best who laughs last. c. People in glasshouses shouldn't throw stones. d. Hunger is the best sauce. e. God helps those who help themselves. f. In wine there is truth. g. One man's meat is another man's poison. h. One should strike while the iron is hot. i. Every cloud has a silver lining. j. The early bird catches the worm. k. Empty vessels make the most noise. l. A stitch in time saves nine. m. Make hay while the sun shines. n. A bird in the hand is worth two in the bush. o. Beggars can't be choosers.

## 129. Read the Results! Was passt in die Lücken?

a. *The election was obviously rigged so a _ _ _ _ was ordered.*
b. *The news showed a dramatic _ _ _ _ of the bank robbery.*
c. *It's quite true that many religions believe in _ _ _ _.*
d. *That misunderstanding with the customs official is something I never want to _ _ _ _.*
e. *Jeremy's manager ordered him to _ _ _ _ the entire project.*
f. *We asked our neighbours to _ _ _ _ their extension.*
g. *The football final was a 0-0 draw so it will be _ _ _ _ on Wednesday.*
h. *No it wasn't an original copy, just a _ _ _ _.*
i. *Cynthia has to _ _ _ _ her oral exams in August.*
j. *We're lost so I think we should _ _ _ _ our steps.*
k. *Karen wore a sequinned dress to her class _ _ _ _.*
l. *You should see the pub now, it's completely _ _ _ _.*
m. *After his divorce Donald intends to _ _ _ _.*
n. *My flight to Sydney has one stop in Singapore to _ _ _ _.*

**refuel**
**revamped**
**reunion**
**remarry**
**resit**
**recount**
**reincarnation**
**reconstruction**
**redo**
**retrace**
**reproduction**
**replayed**
**reposition**
**relive**

## 130. A COMPLETE IDIOM Ergänzen Sie das passende Verb!

a. *Doctor, this child is sick, she's _____ a temperature of 102 degrees!*
b. *That Alan guy has a huge appetite, he _____ like a horse.*
c. *Here comes the boss, I guess it's time to _____ the music.*
d. *As my mother says, there's no use _____ over spilt milk.*
e. *That restaurant was terrible, our meals really _____ a lot to be desired.*
f. *That's right, Jane and Glenn really _____ it off with one another.*
g. *Money is tight at the moment and we're finding it difficult to _____ ends meet.*
h. *We have to _____ while the iron is hot, so we're leaving tonight.*
i. *The hotel we stayed in Boston wasn't anything to _____ home about.*
j. *Ed likes talking so much, it takes him hours to _____ to the point.*
k. *Pauline is a lovely woman, she'd _____ over backwards for you.*
l. *Colm, I have a bone to _____ with you! Where is my bike gone?*

**bend**
**pick**
**strike**
**come**
**make**
**running**
**write**
**eats**
**crying**
**face**
**hit**
**left**

Lösung 131: a. year b. top c. Which d. marks e. sending f. expensive g. local h. teaching i. strict j. A-levels k. afterwards l. degree m. place n. subjects o. hard

Lösung 130: a. running b. eats c. face d. crying e. left f. hit g. make h. strike i. write j. come k. bend l. pick

## 131. A GOOD EDUCATION Ergänzen Sie die passenden Wörter!

| | | |
|---|---|---|
| a. | *Which _ _ _ _ is your son in?* | **subjects** |
| b. | *He's in the _ _ _ _ class at primary school.* | **degree** |
| c. | *_ _ _ _ school does he want to go to?* | **A-levels** |
| d. | *If his _ _ _ _ are good enough he wants to go to grammar school.* | **strict** |
| e. | *We are thinking about _ _ _ _ him to boarding school.* | **local** |
| f. | *But public schools are very _ _ _ _.* | **sending** |
| g. | *My daughter goes to the _ _ _ _ comprehensive school.* | **which** |
| h. | *Are you satisfied with the _ _ _ _ there?* | **hard** |
| i. | *Yes, we are. The teachers are _ _ _ _, but she had very good results.* | **year** |
| j. | *Next year she is going to do her _ _ _ _.* | **top** |
| k. | *Is she planning to go to university _ _ _ _?* | **marks** |
| l. | *She wants to do a _ _ _ _ in business administration and languages.* | **expensive** |
| m. | *Will it be difficult to get a _ _ _ _?* | **teaching** |
| n. | *Yes, she will need very good grades in all _ _ _ _.* | **afterwards** |
| o. | *But if she studies _ _ _ _ enough it shouldn't be a problem.* | **place** |

## 132. TALKING BUSINESS Was passt in die Lücken?

a. *It's time to start our meeting. I would like to _ _ _ _ you to Ms. Marlow.*
b. *First of all I would like us to agree on the day's _ _ _ _.*
c. *Our main _ _ _ _ should be to sign this contract.*
d. *I agree with you but I would also like to _ _ _ _ other possibilities.*
e. *It is important to find a solution that is _ _ _ _ for both sides.*
f. *It will be impossible for us to operate within the time frame you _ _ _ _.*
g. *We will have to extend the _ _ _ _ by at least two weeks.*
h. *If this is the case, we won't be able to pay you the _ _ _ _ we agreed on.*
i. *I'm sorry, but we have already planned our _ _ _ _ on the old figures.*
j. *May I suggest a _ _ _ _?*
k. *We could settle on a lower fee, if you gave us the _ _ _ _ for your next campaign.*
l. *We would be prepared to accept your offer if we could have that in _ _ _ _.*
m. *Agreed. Have we _ _ _ _ everything now?*
n. *Yes, I believe so. _ _ _ _ we'll discuss it in our next meeting.*
o. *Thank you very much for your _ _ _ _ and see you next week.*

**otherwise**
**writing**
**contract**
**compromise**
**fee**
**cooperation**
**deadline**
**acceptable**
**discuss**
**agenda**
**introduce**
**objective**
**proposed**
**budget**
**covered**

Lösung 133: a. find b. pleasant c. meet d. immediately e. hear f. terrible g. someone h. alright i. turn j. think k. honest l. moody m. difficult n. common o. way

Lösung 132: a. introduce b. agenda c. objective d. discuss e. acceptable f. proposed g. deadline h. fee i. budget j. compromise k. contract l. writing m. covered n. Otherwise o. cooperation

## 133. GOSSIP Welche Wörter sind gesucht?

a. *How did you _ _ _ _ _ _ the party on Saturday night?*
b. *Oh, it was very _ _ _ _ _ _.*
c. *Did you _ _ _ _ _ _ Joe's new girlfriend?*
d. *Yes, I did. She's lovely. We hit it off _ _ _ _ _ _.*
e. *But did you _ _ _ _ _ _ about what happened to her?*
f. *Yes, it's _ _ _ _ _ _, isn't it.*
g. *How can _ _ _ _ _ _ be so misfortunate!*
h. *Is she going to be _ _ _ _ _ _ again?*
i. *Oh, yes. It looks like things will _ _ _ _ _ _ out well after all.*
j. *And what do you _ _ _ _ _ _ of Joe himself?*
k. *Well, to be _ _ _ _ _ _, I can't stand him.*
l. *He's a very _ _ _ _ _ _ _ person, don't you think?*
m. *It's very _ _ _ _ _ to get to know him. But he has his good sides.*
n. *I get on well with him, though we don't have much in _ _ _ _ _.*
o. *He really went out of his _ _ _ _ _ _ to help me.*

**turn**
**way**
**common**
**difficult**
**moody**
**think**
**alright**
**terrible**
**immediately**
**meet**
**pleasant**
**find**
**hear**
**someone**
**honest**

## 134. A Car Accident Was passt in die Lücken?

a. *Just ______ at that car. Oh god... it's overturned!*
b. *Is anybody hurt? Jack, you'd better ______ here and help.*
c. *I'll phone for an ______.*
d. *Emergency 999. Which ______, please?*
e. *We need an ambulance. There's been a car ______ in Dawson street.*
f. *What ______ are you ringing from?*
g. *Hold on, I'm ______ from a shop. .. Here it is: 389 685.*
h. *There are people hurt. You have to come ______.*
i. *Can you please tell me what exactly ______?*
j. *A car was going around the corner, it came off the road and ______.*
k. *How many ______were in the car?*
l. *Two. The guy who was driving and a woman in the ______ seat.*
m. *Is anybody ______?*
n. *The driver ____ to have a head injury. The woman was still stuck in the car.*
o. *We'll send out an ambulance at ______. It'll be there in 5 minutes.*

**once**
**passenger**
**people**
**overturned**
**happened**
**phoning**
**crash**
**ambulance**
**stay**
**look**
**service**
**number**
**seems**
**quickly**
**injured**

Lösung 135: a. nice b. chair c. feeling d. hurt e. pain f. pretty g. need h. hope i. lucky j. worse k. doubt l. stay m. operation n. keep o. time

Lösung 134: a. look b. stay c. ambulance d. service e. crash f. number g. phoning h. quickly i. happened j. overturned k. people l. passenger m. injured n. seems o. once

## 135. A Visit at the Hospital

Wie muss es heißen?

| | | |
|---|---|---|
| a. | *Hello Wendy, it's really _ _ _ _ of you to come and see me.* | **time** |
| b. | *Hold on, I'll just grab a _ _ _ _. How are you Diana?* | **operation** |
| c. | *I'm _ _ _ _ much better, thank goodness.* | **stay** |
| d. | *Does it still _ _ _ _?* | **doubt** |
| e. | *My leg is giving me quite a bit of _ _ _ _ and I've got a headache.* | **hope** |
| f. | *I'm worried about my eye. It looks _ _ _ _ ugly, doesn't it?* | **need** |
| g. | *Well, just a bit unusual. But I'm sure there's no _ _ _ _ to worry.* | **hurt** |
| h. | *The doctor say's it'll be fine. I _ _ _ _ he's right.* | **feeling** |
| i. | *Just don't worry. Think how _ _ _ _ you were!* | **chair** |
| j. | *Things could have been much _ _ _ _, couldn't they?* | **nice** |
| k. | *Yes, no _ _ _ _ about that. The accident still was a terrible shock.* | **pain** |
| l. | *How long do you have to _ _ _ _ in hospital?* | **pretty** |
| m. | *Well, they think they might have to do another _ _ _ _ on my leg.* | **lucky** |
| n. | *They want to _ _ _ _ me here for at least three weeks.* | **worse** |
| o. | *That's an awful long _ _ _ _, especially with the hospital food!* | **keep** |

## 136. Grocery Shopping Welche Sätze passen am besten zusammen?

| | |
|---|---|
| a. *Where do you buy your groceries?* | 1. *Really? I'm terribly sorry.* |
| b. *Do you also buy your bread there?* | 2. *I always go to the butcher's in main street.* |
| c. *Where do you buy your meat?* | 3. *Yes, we do. Beef or pork?* |
| d. *What would you like?* | 4. *Sorry, they must have run out.* |
| e. *Do you have any mince meat?* | 5. *No, I prefer to get it fresh from the baker's.* |
| f. *Anything else?* | 6. *Usually I go to the supermarket.* |
| g. *Could I have half a dozen eggs please.* | 7. *No, we only sell whole loafs.* |
| h. *I can't seem to find any tomatoes.* | 8. *Yes, the weighing scales are over there.* |
| i. *Do you sell sliced bread?* | 9. *No thanks, I have some boxes here.* |
| j. *Can you tell me where the pet food is?* | 10. *Certainly. Free-range or organic?* |
| k. *Do I have to weigh the vegetables myself?* | 11. *No. That's everything. Thanks.* |
| l. *How much do I owe you?* | 12. *Yes, you get 10 p back per bottle.* |
| m. *Sorry, I think you've short-changed me.* | 13. *That's 21 pounds 75 altogether.* |
| n. *Is there a deposit on these bottles?* | 14. *Yes, it's in the third aisle on the top shelf.* |
| o. *Would you like a plastic bag?* | 15. *I'd like two pounds of apples, please.* |

Lösung 137: a. car park b. traffic warden c. impossible to find d. parking e. double yellow line f. clamping g. parking rate h. receipt i. manager j. double-parking k. steering wheel lock l. disabled drivers m. long-term n. surcharge o. attendant

Lösung 136: a. 6 b. 5 c. 2 d. 15 e. 3 f. 11 g. 10 h. 4 i. 7 j. 14 k. 8 l. 13 m. 1 n. 12 o. 9

## 137. LOOKING FOR A PARKING SPOT Wie muss es heißen?

| | |
|---|---|
| a. *I think that we need the security of leaving the car in a supervised _______.* | **receipt** |
| b. *Uh-oh, I think I see a person by our car dressed a lot like a _______!* | **impossible to find** |
| c. *If we don't park near the lifts, I feel the car will be _______.* | **double yellow line** |
| d. *Would you prefer we parked outside by a _______ meter?* | **attendant** |
| e. *I think it's safe to park on the _______ after 8 p.m.* | **traffic warden** |
| f. *Dublin Corporation runs a very strict policy of _______ illegally parked cars.* | **disabled drivers** |
| g. *I think that the surcharge at the hotel car park is twice the normal _______.* | **steering wheel lock** |
| h. *Wait here until the machine prints your _______.* | **clamping** |
| i. *I'll ask the _______ if there's a 24-hour car park in the vicinity.* | **surcharge** |
| j. *Oh look, that car has been clamped for _______.* | **car park** |
| k. *I wonder should we buy ourselves a _______ for security?* | **parking rate** |
| l. *We can't park in this space, it's for _______ only.* | **long-term** |
| m. *If we fly to Amsterdam, we can leave our car in the _______ car park.* | **parking** |
| n. *I'm afraid that there's a _______ of five pounds per day.* | **double-parking** |
| o. *We should report that man to the _______.* | **manager** |

## 138. In the Supermarket Was passt in die Lücken?

| | |
|---|---|
| a. Oh, I need small change for a shopping ______. | trolley |
| b. Dean, could you find me the ______ disposable nappies. | shopping list |
| c. I think that the meat department is running a special _____ on lamb chops this week. | off license |
| d. If I buy more than £10 worth of chicken, I'm entitled to 20 points on my ______. | cashier |
| e. Could you get me some coleslaw at the ______? | counter |
| f. I need to get a few bottles of wine at the ______? | bag |
| g. There is a special reduction on brand-name butter, but I need a ______. | delivered |
| h. I think I have everything that was on the ______ list. | assistant |
| i. Dean has to go to football training so we'll use the quick check out ______. | voucher |
| j. Don't eat those crisps now, you'll ruin your appetite. Pack them away in a _____. | discount |
| k. Mummy, the ______ says you have 300 points on your clubcard. | clubcard |
| l. We have too many bags to take on the bus, can we have our shopping ______? | promotion |
| m. Where can I find the ______ washing powders? | brandname |
| n. Why don't you pay for the meat at the ______? | checkout |
| o. Whenever I can't find what I need I ask a shop ______. | deli |

Lösung 139: l - i - n - b - f - o - a - j - c - g - e - d - k - m - h

Lösung 138: a. trolley b. discount c. promotion d. clubcard e. deli f. off-licence g. voucher h. shopping i. counter j. bag k. cashier l. delivered m. brandname n. checkout o. assistant

## 139. SHOPPING FOR CLOTHES Bringen Sie den Dialog in die richtige Reihenfolge!

a. *What about this one then? I think it would suit you very well.*
b. *Yes, I am looking for a black one to wear to a dinner party.*
c. *The fitting rooms are over there.*
d. *Hm, it's a bit wide around the hips. Maybe I need a smaller size.*
e. *There's a big one over here, madam.*
f. *How about this one? It's a very popular style at the moment.*
g. *Thank you. ...Is there a mirror?*
h. *Yes of course. Would you like to follow me to the cash desk, please?*
i. *Yes, I'm looking for a dress.*
j. *Yes, I like it. Can I try it on?*
k. *I'm afraid we haven't any left in size 10. Would you like to try on another model?*
l. *Can I help you?*
m. *No. I think I'll take this one after all. Do you accept credit cards?*
n. *Did you have anything particular in mind?*
o. *No, I think it's a bit too short for me.*

## 140. What a Bargain! Füllen Sie die Lücken!

a. *That's a lovely dress you are _ _ _ _ _.*
b. *Thank you. I only _ _ _ _ _ it yesterday.*
c. *_ _ _ _ _ did you buy it?*
d. *I got it in a clearance _ _ _ _ _ at Arnott's. It was a real _ _ _ _ _.*
e. *Why, how much did it _ _ _ _ _?*
f. *It was only 39.99 together with a _ _ _ _ _ jacket.*
g. *That's very good _ _ _ _ _ for money!*
h. *Do you have to get it _ _ _ _ _ cleaned?*
i. *No, I think you can _ _ _ _ _ wash it separately.*
j. *Oh, that's _ _ _ _ _. Did they have any more of them?*
k. *No, I think I got the _ _ _ _ _ one.*
l. *Oh, that's a _ _ _ _ _!*
m. *But I think they had some left in _ _ _ _ _ colours.*
n. *I definitely have to go and _ _ _ _ _ it out.*
o. *But _ _ _ _ _ up, because the sale ends next week.*

**different**
**pity**
**last**
**hurry**
**machine**
**value**
**cost**
**check**
**where**
**wearing**
**bought**
**sale, bargain**
**matching**
**dry**
**practical**

Lösung 140: a. wearing b. bought c. Where d. sale, bargain e. cost f. matching g. value h. dry i. machine j. practical k. last l. pity m. different n. check o. hurry